Best wishes
Harry Eew

HARRY EDWARDS:
THIRTY YEARS A SPIRITUAL HEALER

Books by Harry Edwards:

Spirit Healing
The Healing Intelligence
The Power of Spiritual Healing
A Guide to Spirit Healing
The Evidence for Spirit Healing
The Mediumship of Jack Webber

HARRY EDWARDS: THIRTY YEARS A SPIRITUAL HEALER

President: The National Federation of Spiritual Healers

THE SPIRITUAL HEALER PUBLISHING CO., LTD
BURROWS LEA, SHERE, SURREY

First published by
Herbert Jenkins Ltd.
2, Clement's Inn,
London, W.C.2
1968

© Harry Edwards 1968

Second Impression 1968

Third Impression 1972

All rights reserved

S.B.N. 257 65788 6
**PRINTED IN GREAT BRITAIN
BY THE ANCHOR PRESS LTD
TIPTREE, ESSEX**

CONTENTS

	FOREWORD BY BEVERLEY NICHOLS	9
	PREFACE	11

Chapter

1.	THE FIRST SIGNS OF THE HEALING GIFT	15
2.	THE FIRST HEALINGS	23
3.	AFTER THIRTY YEARS	31
4.	EMINENT PATIENTS	36
5.	HEALING WITH DOCTORS	43
6.	HEALING IN CYPRUS	52
7.	CLASH WITH A SURGEON	57
8.	THE HEALING OF ANIMALS	62
9.	AN EXPERIMENT IN MASS HEALING	66
10.	MIRACLE IN SURREY	68
11.	HEALING IN STRANGE PLACES	79
12.	THE LESSON OF THE V1 BOMB	85
13.	DISTANCE NO OBJECT	90
14.	EVIDENTIAL HEALING	97
15.	A DOCTOR TESTIFIES	107
16.	SPIRITUAL HEALING AND CHILDBIRTH	110
17.	THE HEALING OF A SCULPTOR'S LIMBS	114
18.	PUBLIC HEALING DEMONSTRATIONS	118
19.	"I THOUGHT I'D NEVER KNIT AGAIN"	123
20.	MY DREAM CAME TRUE AT LAST	127
21.	SPIRITUAL HEALING CAN MISLEAD DOCTORS	130
22.	SPIRITUAL HEALING IS ALL-EMBRACING	133
23.	WHY SOME HEALINGS ARE SAID TO FAIL	136
24.	THIRTY YEARS	147
	POSTSCRIPT	160
	INDEX	165

LIST OF PLATES

Facing Page

1. Platform—at Royal Festival Hall
   Supported by the white-coated members of the National Federation of Spiritual Healers, Harry Edwards addresses the gathering   76
2. The Healing Team
   Ray Branch: Joan Branch: Harry Edwards: Olive Burton: George Burton   77
3. The Healing Sanctuary, Burrows Lea, Shere, Guildford, Surrey   92
4. After a few minutes' healing an "incurable" is able to walk unaided   93
5. The healing of the crippled blind man at Royal Albert Hall   124
6. The healing of a chronic-arthritic woman at a Southampton Healing Service   125
7. Another healing of an arthritic sufferer: note the hands before and after treatment   140
8. Checking the morning's post of absent healing letters   141

FOREWORD

by

BEVERLEY NICHOLS

To call Harry Edwards a "Star Healer of the Spirit World" may sound inappropriate, for in these days the word "star" is usually associated with the world of entertainment. But the phrase can stand. There are "star" healers just as there are "star" composers, poets, actors and actresses. All these men and women have been touched by the divine spark, which has a habit of glittering in very unexpected places, and lighting fires of infinite variation.

Harry, most assuredly, has that spark, and the lives of tens of thousands of suffering people have been lightened by it. From time to time, as one goes through the world, one meets men and women who seem to have an inner radiance. They seem, quite literally, to "shine", and one has the sense that they would even go on shining in the dark. Harry has this radiance to a superlative degree. Throughout our long friendship we have often argued about the channels through which it is directed, and the "techniques" by which they are controlled. Sometimes, in these arguments, we have agreed to differ. The whole subject of healing is so vast and so mysterious that it would be foolish to endeavour to formulate too precise an explanation for every phenomenon. The only things that one can say with certainty are that the source is a Divine one, and that the results are often, quite literally, miraculous.

I would like to think that this book might have a very wide circulation, and not only among the converted. We live in an age when astronomical sums of money are being poured out by the Welfare State in an increasingly arduous effort to cope with the ills of an ailing nation. The nation does not seem to be getting very much healthier, to put it very mildly indeed. And yet here, under our very noses, we have incontestable evidence of a source of healing which is totally neglected by the powers that be. Is it not time that those powers paid it rather more than a passing attention? Is it not indeed vital that orthodox medicine—which is the only sort of medicine recognized by the State—should really examine that evidence, put it to the test, and act on it? Harry would be the first to welcome the most ruthless scrutiny. So would the many honourable spiritual healers with whom he is associated. He, and they, have a great gift to offer to our country, and to the world. How much longer must we wait before we are prepared to accept it?

PREFACE

I WAS invited to write this book at the suggestion of my publishers, but although a mass of evidence of the cures effected through spiritual healing has accumulated throughout my thirty years in this field I have not found it easy to present it in such a form as would avoid monotony. When a doctor first successfully implanted a plastic valve in a human heart, and when the first Sputnik journeyed in space, they became world-wide events, sensationally reported in banner headlines in the world's Press; but as these and other marvels of our age have been repeated, so they have become "ordinary" and less newsworthy.

Thus, to read about one healing "miracle" is exciting, but to run through a whole succession of such miracles (and there have indeed been many, the word "miracle" being more often than not used by doctors who have confirmed extraordinary recoveries) would tend to be boring. I have, therefore, tried to avoid presenting a catalogue of outstanding healings, phenomenal though they may be, but have used them to exemplify the various kinds of spiritual healing, sustaining the human interest by relating the accounts of healings given either by the patients themselves or their relatives just as they were told to me at the time. Several of these accounts have appeared in more or less detailed form in one or other of my previous books, but they are repeated here as being relevant to the theme and the purpose of this book.

Woven into the narrative is the continued conflict between Spiritual Healing on the one hand and the Church and Medicine on the other; for while these latter recognise the supernormal nature of the recoveries, they have refused (up to the present, that is) to acknowledge their Spirit origin.

It is surprising that this should be so because the teachings and healing miracles of Jesus with their new concept of "love one another" have led up to spiritual healing as it is practised today. Yet the sway of religion is declining and the influence of the Church is waning. People are no longer willing to accept the claims of religion blindly; they are nevertheless spiritually hungry, as the vast audiences at evangelical missions indicate. Before a truth can be accepted as a truth it must be *demonstrated* that it is so. Thus, in this scientific and materialistic age, spiritual healing demonstrates that Man is a Spiritual Being and that he is in tune with spiritual sources.

When a person is declared to be "incurable" and doomed to die or, at best, told he must "learn to live" with his infirmity, it denotes the limits of human wisdom and skill. It therefore becomes apparent when, through the application of purposeful spiritual healing, his disease is mastered and he enjoys good health for the remainder of his normal life, then a non-human factor has entered into the picture.

Every healing must be a planned act. The diversity of diseases demands intelligent diagnosis and appropriate treatment. To carry out a plan needs intelligent direction and if that intelligence is not human then it can only be of the Spirit.

It is a simple fact that there must always be a state of attunement between that which is transmitted and that which is received. Thus, the fact that a human sufferer is able to receive help from Spirit forces shows that he must be in attunement with them and their source. In this way, therefore, spiritual healing demonstrates the truth that we are all part Spirit, and furthermore that this life is but a preparatory phase of our future Spirit existence. Spiritual healing proves Man's immortality beyond all reasonable doubt.

What of healers themselves? They certainly are not more knowledgeable than our medical scientists, neither do they know just how the primary causes and effects of incurable conditions are overcome, for the simple reason that, of themselves, they do not do the actual healing—they are but the attuned channels of Spirit, used as "transmitters" of particularised healing forces to effect beneficial changes in given ill-conditions.

It is not the purpose of this book to engage in theological argument or to dispute with the medical profession, but simply to record *facts*. Many of the cases I have cited have been verified medically and supported in writing by the patients themselves.

PREFACE

Every day my postbag brings stories of triumph over physical and mental affliction through the power of spiritual healing which I believe to be God's gift to all His people, irrespective of race or creed. Spiritual healing is not the prerogative of any man or any Church, and neither is it a "cure-all", for even as there are laws which govern the Universe itself, so spiritual healing is governed by certain laws. It is upon this point that I differ with the views of the Church, for the latter so often has it that a healing arises from the personal intervention of God, overriding His laws of creation in favour of a particular man, woman or child. I have never accepted this, but I do, however, believe that spiritual healings are carried out by God's Ministers in Spirit who can operate within the scope of the natural laws to overcome the disharmonies in the mind, body and soul of man.

January 1968

The Sanctuary,
Burrows Lea,
Shere,
Surrey.

CHAPTER ONE

THE FIRST SIGNS OF THE HEALING GIFT

AT the age of fourteen I was apprenticed for seven years to the printing trade as a compositor on the *Field* and *Queen* newspapers. The First World War was two months old when I finished my time, and in the week following I volunteered for war service, enlisting in the 2/6th Cyclist Battalion of The Royal Sussex Regiment.

In 1915 the Battalion moved to Bangalore in southern India, where I initiated and edited *The Royal Sussex Herald*. Then the wheels of destiny began to revolve. The Brigade was ordered to the North-West Frontier to take part in the Mahsud Campaign. The day before we were to move off into action I was instructed to go south to Kirkee, near Bombay, because I was a "printer". I was transferred to the 2nd Battalion of the King's Own Sappers and Miners—the Indian Army equivalent of the Royal Engineers. Then my turn came to proceed to General Headquarters of the Mesopotamian Expeditionary Force in Baghdad, to join the printing section there.

I must confess that my heart was never in print and even during my apprenticeship I did all I could to dodge the column. Thus, on arrival in Baghdad, I looked for something different to do.

I found it, and without going into a long explanation, I succeeded so well, that one evening I was told to report to the Camp Commandant at General Headquarters. I was told to wait and was standing in the spacious foyer of the Residency building, when I saw General Marshall coming down the staircase. When half-way down he stopped, looked at me, and said: "Corporal Edwards?" I came to attention as he continued: "Would you like a commission?" Taken utterly by surprise, I said: "Yes, sir." That was how I was Commissioned in the Field, being a corporal one day and a cadet officer the next, and until the commission was ratified in Orders.

Being commissioned was one thing, but what to do with me was another. My military category was that of a Sapper and Miner, so I was told to report to the Commandant of the Royal Engineers at the Advanced Headquarters in Tekrit. In my interview I was not asked what engineering qualifications I had; they were taken for granted, even though they were nil.

For my first engineering task, I was ordered to lay a railway track to link up two sections of the vital Baghdad to Mosul railway. I was given charge of a labour force consisting of scores of wild nomadic Arabs but, though not lacking in manpower, the one man I needed more than anyone else was an interpreter; I soon discovered that I had to manage without one. Fortunately, the Arabs, seeing the huge accumulation of iron railway sleepers and rails, appreciated what had to be done and the work began. The clang of hammers on iron was frequently punctuated by cries of pain. Thumbs were smashed, feet crushed and heads knocked as my inexperienced gangers wielded their heavy hammers, but gradually the track grew until finally it was completed. I must confess that I always felt a little hurt afterwards, for never did I see a train go over my particular section at more than five miles an hour!

My most noteworthy engineering feat at Tekrit was the building of the camp incinerator. It was circular in shape and about twenty feet in diameter. I built the wall up with bricks made of mud and straw, about four feet high and then thought if I gradually placed the bricks inwards, I should be able to enclose it. What I did not appreciate at the time was how long the roofing process would take; it went up and up, higher and higher, until it towered over the plain like a great monument. It was called the "Edwards Mosque".

It was there that I did my first "surgical" healing. The son of the Mohammedan priest (the Mullah) had an abcess in the sole of his foot. The feet of Arabs are unique, for their long barefoot journeys over the sandy desert result in the soles of the feet becoming very hard, almost bone-like, with a hard skin a quarter of an inch thick. Sometimes this skin develops very deep fissures and in the case of the boy it was behind this layer of thick, hardened skin that the abcess had formed.

I am extremely squeamish at the sight of wounds, and even flinch at taking a splinter from a finger with the aid of a needle. I think it was the bravest act I ever did when I took a thin razor-blade between my fingers and with my nerves tensed up, made a deep incision into the sole of that foot to lance the abcess and clean it out. To my surprise, the boy said he felt no pain and the foot was soon well again. He must have sensed some deep kind of friendly bond between us, for he asked to become my "servant for life".

From Tekrit I was sent to Persia to build roads and bridges and it was during this time that quite unknowing to myself, the gift of healing found its expression. It was only in later years that I realized spiritual healing had been in operation.

North-western Persia (now called Iran) is a land of mountains and valleys. The existing roads at that time were nothing more than sandy tracks, with narrow pathways up through the mountains just sufficient for horses, camels and donkeys to find their way over. New metalled roads and bridges had to be constructed to carry the heavy military lorries, guns and transports. The only assistance I had was a couple of British soldiers and the local Persians. I was given shovels, pickaxes, hammers and hand rammers. When I sent out a call for local labour men, women and children, came in by the hundreds and thousands, from the surrounding villages.

At one place I needed to build a bridge over a wide fast-running river. At first this appeared to my untrained mind an impossible task. I solved the problem by building a stone bridge on dry land adjacent to the river-bed, and when it was finished the river was diverted to flow under it. It was completely successful.

Twice Persia had been ravaged by war. The Russians had pushed the Turks back to the borders who then, reinforced with German troops, drove the Russians back to the Caspian Sea. As a result, Persia was laid bare. There had been no harvests, all the animals had been killed and the people were dying from starvation.

So it was that those who came in response to the call for workers were so weak they could do no work at all. We fed them until they were able to take what donkeys they had to the mountains to bring back stone and to prepare the foundations for the road, dig the drainage ditches and so on.

They had to use the tools we provided, so very different from their own primitive kind, and, as with my Arab labour force they were unaccustomed to using them, so that it was not surprising that a man with a pickaxe would hit another worker with it, and the women breaking up the larger stones would hit a thumb with the hammer instead of the stone. So they came to me with all sorts of injuries.

All the medical supplies I had were bandages, iodine and castor oil. It was noted, however, by the Persians and myself how quickly the wounds healed, sometimes overnight. At that time I attributed this to the hardness of the people and their natural recuperative powers, but even so I earned a new title being known as the "hakim" or healer.

As my reputation grew the people would tell me, through an interpreter, of their sicknesses and afflictions. I knew little or nothing about them and the only "treatment" I was able to give, was a dose of castor oil. I remember being surprised at the results, for it seemed that I only had to be told about their troubles and give a spoonful of castor oil for relief to be brought about.

The local ideas of medicine were unusual to say the least. A woman with a bad thumb once came to me with a lizard split open along its abdomen and impaled on her thumb; and I recall a man who had been hit on the face with a pickaxe arriving with his face covered with some black substance which I found out was a mixture of donkey's blood and ink! The ink had come from a written extract from the Koran, which a mullah had written and then washed it off into the donkey's blood.

My fame as a "hakim" spread, and all kinds of people came out to see me in my camp on the plains or in the hills. I did not question why people got well, for I accepted it simply as a matter of course, without wondering why it was.

One morning a nearby Sheik with a mounted escort came to my tent. He had brought his aged mother who was wedged into a pannier on one side of a mule; another female sat in another pannier on the other side to give balance. The son told me his mother was very ill, weak, and could not eat and that she also had strong internal pains. When I looked at her, I could see she was ill indeed and very, very old, her deeply lined and wrinkled face told its story of her advanced age. I was expected to make her well.

THE FIRST SIGNS OF THE HEALING GIFT

Even to my inexperienced eyes, the case seemed hopeless; but I had to do something, for if I did not, the Sheik would have been upset and he could have made much trouble. I had to improvise, so I went into my tent, where I had some pink carbolic tooth powder (army issue), and put four small pinches of the tooth powder into four paper spills. I told the Sheik to give one to his mother in a little water at sunrise and another at sunset for the next two days, and off the cavalcade went.

Three mornings later I was going about my duties in the camp when I saw a score of horsemen armed with rifles galloping towards me. When they fired their rifles in the air, I thought for a moment I was being attacked—I did not then know the firing of the rifles was a friendly salute. My interpreter had fled. The horsemen, led by the Sheik whose mother I had "treated" halted a few yards away. He dismounted and walked towards me. I called for my interpreter who had been hiding in my tent, and although very frightened he came out and listened to what the Sheik had to say. When I saw the Sheik and his men laughing together I knew all was well. He had come to express his thanks for my making his mother well; she had no more pains and was eating again.

The Sheik wanted to pay me and asked what I would like. He offered me a bag of gold Turkish lira, but I refused this saying that I was happy to have helped his mother, and this was all the thanks I wanted. The Sheik was not satisfied with this, so he said he would bring some carpets, I again told him I did not wish for any reward, but he went on insisting. I saw that he would be offended if I did not take something, so I said to him: "If you have any eggs for my breakfast they would be welcome." This pleased him and he rode away with his escort. That afternoon he returned with baskets containing over three hundred eggs.

On other occasions I came up against religious prejudice. Perhaps that was just a foretaste of what was to come years later. A mother brought her little baby only a few months old. It was a poor little thing, wizened and weak. I had no idea what was wrong; the baby looked as if it was dying.

I remember feeling surprised that the mother, a local woman, unlettered and primitive should bother to bring her baby for help, because life is not valued very highly, especially female babies, and suffering generally is treated with indifference. However, I took the baby and held it to myself for a few moments and prepared and gave it a few small spoonfuls of condensed milk in water. I had little hope that the baby would live.

The next afternoon the mother returned with the baby and to my disgust I saw the baby's mouth was filled with grass. My interpreter told me that when the mother got back to her village, the baby had stopped crying, had slept through the night and had taken food that morning. The mullah heard about this and was very angry that the woman had gone to an unbeliever, an infidel, and said I had given the baby to the devil. So he had filled the baby's mouth with grass, as his method of exorcising the "evil", and thereby the baby's sickness. For some unexplained reason the mother turned her back on her priest and again brought the baby to me.

I was in a quandary, for I did not want the mother to bear the mullah's displeasure, which I knew could be so extreme as to kill both the mother and child. I took the grass out of the baby's mouth and gave it some more milk and water, and sent them in my Ford van to our hospital in Kermanshah with an explanatory letter to the medical officer.

Later, I heard from the doctor. He had kept the mother and child for a week or two; the baby was better, taking nourishment and putting on some weight and in consultation with the political officer arranged for both mother and baby to be accepted into another community some distance away.

There was another occasion when I came into conflict with the mullahs, though this was not a case of healing. I was quartered in Kermanshah at the time. The colonel under whom I was serving had an Indian Christian batman who had just married a local Mohammedan girl. The head mullah took exception to this, sending his men who took the girl by force and imprisoned her in the mosque. It was a difficult situation and my colonel did not wish to take action for political reasons, but asked me if I could do something about it.

I had a letter written in flowery language to the mullah, saying that as the girl was married to an Indian soldier, she was now a subject of His Majesty King George, the Emperor of India, and asking for the girl to be released. This was of no avail and the reply was that she had been sentenced to death by stoning. What happens on these occasions is that the prisoner is buried up to the waist in a pit and stones are hurled at the unfortunate being until death takes place. Then the stones are built up round the body into a cairn, as a warning to others.

I could only try a bluff. My interpreter at that time was an Assyrian who had been trained in an American Mission. He had an understanding mind with a sense of humour and the dramatic, and he quite thought he was half an American himself. I also had my own small police force, which was used to protect the Persian labour on the roads from brigands. They looked a fearsome lot, bristling with rifles (which I did not think they could fire), swathes of ammunition belts, curved daggers and so on, and were dressed in khaki uniforms. I chose six of them and gave each one a piece of rope to carry. With the interpreter, I sent them to the mosque and ordered the mullah to come and see me. If he refused, the policemen were to tie him up and bring him by force or as an alternative to bring back the girl. There was no intention to carry out the threat—it was pure bluff, but it worked and they brought the girl back. The crisis passed, although the Indian and his wife were transferred elsewhere to save any further trouble.

The last healing experience I will relate about those times was an unusual one. In Kermanshah, like other Persian cities, the houses had flat roofs with a stairway leading up to it. One could walk along these roofs from one house to another. In the courtyard of each house was a water pool, the water being used for drinking, washing and, indeed, all purposes. The water supply came from the high ground on which the city is built, proceeding from the houses with the highest elevation through an outflow pipe into the pool in the next house lower down and so on, right down through all the houses until it finally reached those at the bottom. As can be imagined, it was a most unhygienic arrangement providing one cause of plague epidemics which often wiped out a high percentage of the inhabitants.

The house next to mine was occupied by a high ranking Persian military officer who had his harem there. I recall causing some embarrassment on one occasion when I went on to the roof of my billet and looked over into the courtyard of the house next door, where I saw the officer's wives bathing in the pool. One looked up and saw me and screamed. I beat a hasty retreat.

One evening I heard continuous heart-rending screams coming from the house next door, and I thought a woman was being murdered. So I went up on to my roof to show myself, hoping it would act as a deterrent. When I looked down I saw a young woman screaming and struggling with the other women who were trying to prevent her from throwing herself into the pool. I could not understand what was wrong.

I descended and sent the interpreter to find out what was happening. Soon he came back and told me that the woman had been stung on the arm by a scorpion. I knew that a scorpion's sting was terribly agonising, almost as if all the circulatory system had become red hot and lasting for a full twenty-four hours. I sent the interpreter back to ask if I could go in and help her. He returned to say that as the officer was away, no one could be permitted to enter.

The screaming continued and I could stand it no longer, so with the interpreter I went and knocked on the garden door. When it opened, I did not hesitate but went in and took the woman's arm, placing my hand firmly over the inflamed centre where she had been stung. Recalling this later, I did not know why I did this—it was intuitive. After a few moments, the woman stopped screaming. She was by now completely exhausted and sank down as if in a deep sleep. She was quiet, so I left her in the care of the other women, who looked at me as if I was a visitor from another world.

I knew that I had committed a grave offence by going into the harem and wondered what would be the outcome. I did not have long to wait. A few days later I was told that the officer from next door asked if he could see me. I agreed and he came into my office in his full military regalia, white coat, blue trousers, revolver in his belt and long sword in its scabbard. "Now for it," I thought, "he's probably going to challenge me to a duel." But there was no trouble at all, for he had come to thank me for what I had done.

There were other instances of unusual healings, but looking back over the years to those of 1917–20, I now know that the healing gift was with me then, though I was quite oblivious as to its origin and nature.

CHAPTER TWO

THE FIRST HEALINGS

IN 1935, a friend who lived in the next road to me told me about her experiences in a small Spiritualist Church in Balham. She had received evidence from a clairvoyant concerning a near relative who had recently passed over from a road accident, and the more we discussed the matter the more we became convinced that the circumstantial evidence my friend received could not possibly have been known by the medium. I felt interested, and so the following week we went along to the "church" which consisted of two ground-floor rooms of a house with the folding doors hinged back.

That evening an "open circle" was being held, and I saw about a score of people seated in a circle, where we also took our places. It was, apparently, a training circle for mediumship.

There is no purpose in relating all that transpired, except that the medium came and stood in front of me and told me that I had been "born to heal" and built up a word picture of the future service I should render to the sick in the years to come. I listened to her attentively, but nevertheless in a sceptical frame of mind, for all that she said seemed highly improbable. Yet in some way my interest was maintained, in spite of my opinion then that Spiritualism was the resort of cranks and the credulous.

However, we continued to visit that little church and attended others. To my surprise, wherever I went I was told by mediums that I was a "healer". I did not even know what a "healer" was. At one meeting, a medium who was later destined to become very well known, gave me a message to the effect that the next time I knew of a person who was sick, I should concentrate my thoughts on that person's recovery.

The opportunity soon came, for a few days later whilst my

friend and I were sitting together in another developing circle, she told me about a friend of hers who knew a man who was dying in Brompton Hospital from advanced tuberculosis (galloping consumption as it was then called) complicated with pleurisy and haemorrhages. I said to her, "Let's try a healing experiment." So we sat quietly in meditation employing our thoughts for his recovery. As I did this, with my eyes closed, I became aware that I was looking down a long hospital ward, with my attention focused on a man in the last bed but one. I was conscious of all the surrounding detail and of the man himself. So strong was this picture that even over thirty years later I can revive it at will in all its vivid detail. When I checked the description of what I had "seen" with a relative of the patient, it was found to be correct in every detail. It proved to be my first experience of "astral travelling".

A week later we received news about this patient and were told that within twenty-four hours of our intercession, the haemorrhages ceased, all pleuretic pains vanished, and his temperature had come down almost to normal. Naturally we were very pleased to learn this. The news continued good, and at the next check it was found that the blood and sputum were free from infection. The doctors were amazed, not being able to account for the man's remarkable recovery from death's door in such a short time. He gained so rapidly in vitality and strength that three weeks after our first intercession he was sent to a convalescent home prior to his discharge. These events occurred in August, and the man was able to resume full employment before the end of the year. We were able to maintain contact with the patient's friend for some years, and in response to all our subsequent enquiries, were told he was in constant good health.

My personal reaction to this healing was one of hesitancy. It was too good to believe, and I could not free my mind from the possibility of other factors having intervened or that it was sheer coincidence that the man had recovered; but these thoughts were dispelled during the next few weeks when two further outstanding cases of healing occurred, which gave me great encouragement.

At that time I had a printing and stationery business in Balham High Road, London, and one afternoon a woman came into the shop, looking very unhappy. Her name was Mrs. Newland and she lived in Coalbrook Mansions nearby. Seeing that she was so upset

THE FIRST HEALINGS

and tearful, I asked if I could help her. She told me she did not know why she had come in, for she had been walking about aimlessly, but as she passed my shop she felt impelled to come in. It was obvious from her demeanour that something was very wrong, and it only needed a little encouragement from me for her to unfold her story . . .

Her husband had been very ill in St. Thomas's Hospital. When she visited him three days before, the doctors had sent for her and told her that her husband was suffering from an incurable cancer on the lung, and that no further medical treatment could be given to him. It would be best for her to have him at home and make him as comfortable as she could until he died. The hospital had sent him home the previous day, and she had felt so distracted and unhappy that she had to go out for a while. This was how she had come to be walking along Balham High Road. I was a little hesitant at first, but decided to take the plunge and tell her about spiritual healing and suggested that I might call round and see her husband. She told me that he did not know why he was so gravely ill and if she took a stranger in to see him, he would get suspicious; moreover, he was an avowed agnostic, so a visit to give him spiritual healing was out of the question. I comforted her as best I could and said I would ask for absent healing to be given to him. That night I went into intercession for healing to help him in every way that could be.

Two days later Mrs. Newland came in to see me again. She was smiling and looked a different woman. She related how the previous morning (that is, the morning after I had entered into intercession), her husband had got up, made her an early morning cup of tea, and had taken it in to her. This in itself was a most unusual thing for him to do, but it was the wonderful change in him which was so remarkable. He no longer seemed weak; he had no pain, and there was colour in his face as if he was glowing with health.

Later that day she had arranged for their children to come and sit by their father's bedside, in case that might be their last opportunity of seeing him alive. Instead of this, they found him up and about and they could only marvel at the change that had come to him. Thus it was, that she had come to see me, and give thanks for her husband's healing, for she knew that there could be no other possible reason to account for it.

After his recovery, Mr. Newland went back to St. Thomas's Hospital to ask the doctor to sign him off for work. His own doctor was not there at that time and so he saw another doctor, who sent for Mr. Newland's medical history, which included X-ray photographs that showed the cancer. The doctor, however, could not believe that Mr. Newland had had lung cancer. He was convinced that the patient before him could not possibly have been the same man that the medical history referred to; if he was, then the X-ray photographs had been wrongly labelled. Still very puzzled, the doctor signed Mr. Newland off as fit for light work.

This man lived for many years afterwards and I recall seeing his name featured in a national daily newspaper as a maker of hand-made violins. I invited Mr. and Mrs. Newland to my sixtieth birthday dinner in 1953; eighteen years had passed since he was so ill. Mrs. Newland attended but Mr. Newland could not as he was then troubled with arthritis. It was a mystery to me why Mrs. Newland had not again asked for our help to see what healing could do for the arthritis. Perhaps the reason was that Mr. Newland was still an agnostic.

The strange way in which Mrs. Newland was induced to seek my help for her husband was repeated with the third case, that of Miss Gladys Cudd. It may be thought that special Spirit guidance was being directed at this time, with the purpose of not only healing people who were very ill, but also to make me aware of my healing potential, having in view the ministry of healing I was destined to undertake.

Thus it transpired that, a short time after the two cases I have related, a young woman knocked at my door late at night. She told me a remarkable story. Her name was Miss Hetty Cudd, whose sister, Gladys, was very ill. They lived in a near-by road.

Hetty was a Spiritualist and was very concerned about her sister. She sought spiritual healing for her by going to a medium on the other side of London. The medium entered into a trance and the Spirit Guide controlling her told Hetty that she should seek out a Harry Edwards who lived near to her, and to do so that very night. When she got back to Balham she did all she could to try and find out where I lived, but did not succeed until she found the Secretary of the Balham Spiritualist Society, who gave her my address.

THE FIRST HEALINGS

It should be remembered that at that time my name was quite unknown as a healer.

So it was that Hetty knocked at my door at about eleven o'clock that night. I invited her in, and she told me about her sister's illness, that it was feared she would die, and asked if I would go and see her. I promised to do so the next morning and in the meantime I would seek absent healing to reach her.

The next morning I went to the house and on my arrival I saw that straw had been strewn on the road and pavement to deaden the noise of passing traffic (remember, this was thirty years ago) so that nothing would disturb the sick girl. The mother took me upstairs into a darkened room where the girl lay unconscious on her bed.

This was the first sick patient I had ever tried to help by contact healing, I did not know what to do and felt embarrassed and self-conscious. I stood at the head of the bed, behind the black iron rails. I placed my hands through the rails and let them rest lightly on the girl's head. As I asked for healing to reach her, I became conscious of a new experience, for I felt as if I was rooted to the floor, my body alive with "energy", which seemed to possess me and then to flow in a stream down my arms into my hands and thence into the patient. There was no quivering or shaking; I was literally a reservoir of energy that found its outlet through my hands into the sick girl. How long this sensation lasted I do not know, but it seemed a long time before the flow of energy slowly weakened and ceased. I then became conscious of an exalted feeling of happiness and confidence. I was impelled to say to the mother standing by, "She will be up by Sunday." It was then Thursday. Later I learned not to make such prophecies, but did so on that occasion quite spontaneously.

I shall never forget the look of utter disbelief on the mother's face as I said this, and I do not wonder at it, for the mother had told me before we went into her daughter's bedroom that the doctor could not diagnose her daughter's disease, only that he knew she was very ill indeed, and near to death.

When the doctor called that afternoon he found that the high fever had gone and that her temperature was down nearly to normal, a factor he could not understand. The girl was sleeping and she continued to sleep until the next morning (Friday) when, upon waking, she brought up a huge quantity of a red, flesh-like substance. When this vomiting attack was over, she was able to take nourishment comfortably. By Saturday, it was clear that a fantastic change had taken place. She was not distressed at all, her temperature was normal, and apart from general weakness she seemed more like her normal self. On the Sunday afternoon, she got up to have tea with her family in her bedroom. My unbelievable prophecy had turned out to be a true one!

At that time I did not know that Gladys was a consumptive, with one collapsed lung, and I was asked to continue to seek help for her lungs, which I gladly did. Every two weeks she had to go to the hospital for an air-refill for the collapsed lung. On her next visit, the doctors found that her lung had inflated to normal, and though they tried to recollapse it by administering air, they could not get the air to build up the chest cavity. She brought up no more sputum, her temperature remained normal, and all further tests showed that she was free from infection.

I first saw Gladys at the end of August, and it was early in the following year when she returned to the sanatorium, where she had previously been an in-patient, for a thorough medical overhaul. The verdict was that she was completely free from disease, and she was actually accepted as a nurse in the same sanatorium shortly afterwards! I kept in touch with Gladys for many years during which she married and reared a family of healthy children. She had no other illnesses.

Her sister, Hetty, provides another healing story. She had been born with a club foot necessitating the wearing of a surgical boot. From the knee down the leg was extremely wasted, and the foot contracted, with the toes curling underneath it. Both foot and ankle were fixed, and it was impossible for her to get her heel down to the ground.

Despite the seemingly impossible task of readjusting the foot, I recall that even in those early days of my healing work I had abundant confidence in what I was doing and so eagerly sought healing for the deformity by both absent and contact healing. I used to take the foot in my hands, seeking for movement in the ankle and feet bones, and try to bring about some pliability. Gradually, it appeared that the foot was beginning to move up and down; but it was so slight, that I remember questioning

THE FIRST HEALINGS

whether, in fact, there was any new movement. For over a year regularly each month I continued to treat Hetty's foot, and we were delighted to observe progressive movement within the joints and the abnormal shape of the foot gradually lessening. We had proof of this when she needed to have a new boot, for it had to be made to new measurements.

During the second year of treatment, the improvement continued until she was able to stand with both the heel and ball of the 'foot resting on the floor. Finally she was able to discard the surgical boot and wear ordinary shoes. She walked without a limp, and during the war became an ambulance driver, her right foot acting normally and never giving her any further trouble.

There is one more healing case connected with the Cudd family in those early days of my healing ministry.

Mrs. Cudd had a lady friend who was dying from an abdominal cancer. Mrs. Cudd had been so impressed with the healing of her daughters, she asked if I would go with her and visit her friend. I agreed, and one evening we set out to go to Streatham where the patient lived.

Her friend was lying in bed in the downstairs living-room. She was in great pain and her lady doctor was calling four times a day to give her morphia injections. The doctor expected her to pass over any day.

When we went into the rather small room, the husband and children were there, too. With Mrs. Cudd and I it was overcrowded. No one knew why I had come, except as a friend of Mrs. Cudd. There was no mention of healing and, indeed, any reference to it would not have been understood. A more uncongenial atmosphere for a healer to work in would be difficult to imagine, and, as a complete stranger, I felt awkward and embarrassed.

The patient was crying and twisting with pain; the doctor was expected to come at any minute and give another merciful pain-killing injection. I had a chair by the bed, and all that I could do was to hold the patient's hand and, within myself, seek for the peace of healing to come to her. Whilst I was doing this, there was a persistent buzz of conversation and the children were making a noise as well. Soon, there was a knock on the door. The doctor had arrived and we had to go. I felt glad when we left, for it all seemed so impossible.

That night, the patient rectally discharged a copious quantity of abnormal matter. She was no longer in pain and slept well. When morning came, it was clear that something quite remarkable had happened to her. She was bright, cheerful and ate a good breakfast. Her weakness had gone and she had a new vitality. When the doctor called, she was astounded at the change in her patient, and could see that no further injections were needed. A little later on, the district nurse called in as usual to wash the patient and make her comfortable, but the patient refused her services saying she was better and could look after herself. All symptoms, even the swelling of the abdomen, had gone. This lady lived for a number of years afterwards and ultimately passed over from a stroke.

In my keenness, I thought this recovery provided foolproof evidence for spiritual healing, so I arranged with Mrs. Cudd to interview the doctor and her friend to tell them about the healing, in order to get their observations. The doctor said she knew nothing about it and would make no comment, and all the patient said to Mrs. Cudd was: "What, that young man! He only came once."

It was my first rebuff in my endeavours to prove the reality of spiritual healing, and I was not then to know how this was going to be repeated over and over again in the years ahead by the highest medical and ecclesiastical authorities in the land.

Needless to say, after these first healings all my doubts vanished. I accepted spiritual healing as a truth, and though I had much to learn, I entered into the healing work with all my heart.

CHAPTER THREE

AFTER THIRTY YEARS

I AM going to jump thirty years from 1935 to a public healing demonstration held at Bangor in North Wales in November 1964 because it provides an illustration of the progress which has been achieved in the present "way of healing", contrasting with those self-conscious hesitant times I have so far related.

In these latter days, I have commented more than once to my associates, how easily healings take place at public demonstrations. No matter how long a patient has suffered from a crippling disability, such as locked arthritic joints, after a few moments' intercession, I become conscious of a supreme confidence, born of knowing inwardly that the healing has already taken place so that I can tell the patient to move his joints freely—and he can. In the case of an obvious growth that can be felt with the fingers, I know that after a few seconds' attunement, I can ask the patient to see if he can "find it" and usually he cannot, for it has disappeared. Patients who have been in constant pain day and night for some time, find, after healing, that they are no longer in pain.

It is now a common experience to observe the dispersal of goitres and other forms of growths as they quickly yield to the healing touch, especially through that of my colleague George Burton, for it is clear he has a special gift for dispersal of undesirable matter. At public healing services, goitres—some very large—are clearly seen by the many people present to disappear within a very short time under George's fingers.

The facility, therefore, with which we have seen some of the most chronic and obstinate physical conditions yield at these public healing demonstrations has, on rare occasions, led me into the error of being just a little too "cock-sure", and our demonstration at Bangor was an instance of this. This is what happened.

At all these public services I need to deal with afflictions where an immediate improvement can be apparent to the audience, and, to avoid monotony, I seek to cover a wide variety of diseases, such as arthritis, slipped discs, spinal curvatures, paralysis, spastic limbs, deafness, lack of sight, etc.

At Bangor, I had asked for those who had pronounced lateral spinal curvatures to put up their hands and in accordance with my usual custom I selected two persons at random from the audience. One of these was a comparatively young woman, whose age I judged to be about thirty-five. She was stockily built, below average height, and walked with a pronounced limp and twist of the body with each step she made.

It is my custom at these demonstrations, to question patients, using the microphone, and encouraging them to give as full a picture of their trouble as possible for the benefit of the assembly. I enquire about the medical history, the hospitals the patients have been in, what treatment (if any) they are now receiving, and what the prevailing medical diagnosis of the trouble now reveals.

When the young woman arrived on the platform, I asked her to sit down with her back to the audience, and in answer to my questions she said that she had developed the spinal curvature from being dropped at a very young age, after which she had been an inmate of a number of hospitals for varying periods of time. She had not received any medical attention for years, simply because the doctors could not help her and as she did not suffer any pain it was now an "accepted" condition. The curvature had become more pronounced with the passing of time, and the rib distortion had increased as the spine became more twisted and set.

For the benefit of the audience I traced with my finger the shape of the spine from the tilt in the neck, to where the backbone went sideways and disappeared beneath the shoulder-blade emerging below it and then proceed in a transverse direction across the centre of the body forming another curve before it merged into the tilted pelvis. It was like a distorted letter 'S'. I was moved to impress upon the audience the gravity of the condition; how solid the spine had become; and how the tilting of the pelvis caused her to walk with a pronounced limp.

When such a chronic spinal condition comes for treatment, we usually only obtain a partial correction at the first treatment, a number of these being needed over a period of time to induce the maximum benefit that is possible. My mind was aware of this, but on this occasion I acted as if I was expecting an immediate and full recovery. By pointing out all the difficulties of this particular case I was making it much harder for myself, and I have wondered since why I had the effrontery to do this. At these healing services, and indeed at all times when engaged in either contact or absent healing, I am aware of being "over-shadowed" by the spirit guide or doctor, but I am always in full possession of all my faculties and reason. These should have told me that a complete realignment of the spine was most unlikely, and that is why I wondered at my temerity in drawing the attention of the audience to the full gravity of the ill-condition. I can only say that I was intuitively directed to do so.

The healing commenced. I placed one hand over the lumbar vertebrae and asked the young woman to let her spine bend, to yield backwards over my hand and then to bend over forwards so that the spine could bend outwards in the opposite direction. The rigid solidity of the spine yielded and it became mobile. Next, with the assistance of George Burton, I asked the lady to bend the upper part of her body over to the left. With my right hand placed on the right upper part of her body I asked her to let her back straighten upright and as she did this my right hand gently, mildly persuasive, encouraged the straightening up process to bring the spine central and so correct the misalignment.

I then saw she was sitting upright with her head erect. A big change had taken place, but I did not know to what extent until I traced with my fingers the shape of the spine. To my amazement, I found that it now proceeded straight down the centre of the back. The gross curvature had disappeared and the spine was now correctly aligned. The time taken for this to take place was not more than a minute or two.

I told the audience what had transpired and I asked her to feel where her spine now was, and it caused some amusement to those behind me on the platform to see the look of bewilderment on her face as she felt her spine dead centre down her body. Still more significant the rib distortion had also almost gone.

All this time, the woman had been sitting with her back to the audience, so that it could observe a healing in action. I turned her sideways to face me, and still being intuitively directed I said through the microphone so that everyone could hear: "Because your spine is now straight, the pelvic tilt should have gone and your hips be level. Please stand up."

She stood up and felt her hips, and we could all see they were level. The lady excitedly volunteered to say: "Both my feet are flat on the ground, I never remember them being like that before." Previously, owing to the pelvic tilt, one leg appeared shorter than the other.

I asked her to bend over with her legs straight to see how far she could bend her spine in an effort to touch her toes. While she could not get right down, she was able to bend over a good way. After this I told her to "mark time", lifting both knees straight up in front and putting her feet flat down as if she was walking. Then came the final test. I asked her to walk, without limping, and she found she was able to walk normally, without any twisting of the body or any limp.

That is the end of this story, except for this comment. I never heard from that young woman again. There was no word of gratitude from her, nor did she let me know about the permanence of her cure. It may seem strange, but this is usual. At these public demonstrations all over the country, wonderful healings of all kinds of afflictions have been effected, yet it is the rare exception for us to receive a letter afterwards to say "thank you".

This healing story serves to illustrate the greater ease with which healing takes place today. This may arise from the increased wisdom of the spirit doctors themselves in the usage of the healing forces from Spirit; or from their experience in using us as better channels for the healing and possibly our ability through finer attunement to co-operate more closely with them.

It follows that with healing the sick, day by day, a more intimate state of attunement is established with the spirit doctors and we become more co-operative instruments. This theme has been the subject of my last book, *The Healing Intelligence*. The healing of the woman at Bangor supports this, for if my normal judgement had dominated my actions, I certainly would not have drawn the attention of the audience to all the difficulties which were likely to prevent the complete spinal transformation to take place as it did.

AFTER THIRTY YEARS

It seems obvious that the spirit doctors were able to foresee a successful result under the conditions pertaining at the time and therefore influenced my mind to act as it did.

I have just mentioned that the spirit doctors gain more wisdom as time passes; this is a natural development, and to be expected. The freeing of spastic and poker-back spines is now an everyday occurrence with healers everywhere, far more so than, say, ten to fifteen years ago. Every such healing is a planned act and behind the plan must be the knowledgeable minds to carry it out.

Again, contemplate what happened with the woman's back at Bangor. Remember, it was a life-long condition; the spine had become permanently fixed, ossified into a poker-back state; the ribs had grown distorted to conform to the shape of the spine and body; the muscles and tissues had developed to accommodate the mis-shapen body.

Then the spine was straightened, coming from under the shoulder-blade to the centre of the back, which in itself gave her an increase in height and improved posture. For this to have taken place, the rib cage must have altered in shape, and bearing in mind that this houses the lungs and the heart, it is remarkable that no harm was done to these organs. Previously her breathing had been shallow, owing to the contracted and spastic condition of the chest, but with the resulting new shape of the rib cage her breathing at once improved, for her lungs were then able to function correctly. Further consideration indicates that as the spine had become rigid and immovable, the intervertebral discs of cartilage had perished and dried up. These discs must have been restored as a prelude to the restoration of mobility, and the straightening, otherwise the vertebrae would have grated upon each other as the spine moved. Branches of the nerves emerge in pairs from between the vertebrae, and the correction was performed without impinging on these nerves. Thus, it appears that the healing was not limited to the re-alignment of the backbone but embraced anatomical adjustments, too—an "operation". Think what would have been involved surgically! Hours upon the operating table; a team of surgeons . . . I need not go on. It is obvious, and the more one thinks about the implications arising from this healing story, the more wonderful and inexplicable does it become.

CHAPTER FOUR

EMINENT PATIENTS

FROM time to time, I have been asked to give healing treatment to people whose names are known all over the world. These have included members of the British and other Royal Families and rulers of other lands; Peers and Peeresses, Cabinet Ministers, Army Commanders, Judges, Bishops—and an Archbishop; stage, film and television celebrities; a national orchestra conductor; editors and owners of national newspapers, and so on through all levels of society.

No matter who the sick person might be I have always regarded all equal in the sight of healing, and none of those whom I have seen in the past have received any preferential treatment. The only distinction that I have made, in the case of eminent people, is not to receive them at a public healing session at the Sanctuary, where they would be recognised, but either privately beforehand or at some other time convenient to both of us.

Healing treatment of such patients has always been given in the strictest confidence, and I am not free to mention the names of many of these people, who are still living, or any others, without permission.

I can, however, recount the case of one of the most beloved members of our Royal Family who received spiritual healing from us continuously for a number of years until her earthly life ended peacefully. She was Her Royal Highness Princess Marie Louise and she was a frequent visitor to the Sanctuary, accompanied always by her ladies-in-waiting. Olive Burton and I would see her in private session during the morning.

The Princess was receptive to spiritual healing. At first, her main troubles were arthritis in her arms and more acutely in her legs, accompanied by general tiredness and debility. When the arthritis was troublesome, she would walk into the Sanctuary with the aid of a stick or on the arm of a lady-in-waiting. After her healing, she would delight in showing how much better she was by walking freely up and down in the Sanctuary and then, with ease, back to her car.

She was a charming personality and, when she sat down before us for treatment, she would always ask first for absent healing to be directed to other members of the Royal Family and those within her circle of friends before she allowed us to commence healing for her. She would report the progress each of her sick people had made, and at one time was specially concerned for the ex-Queen of Spain. I recall one occasion, when, after she had given us her usual reports, I rather indifferently accepted them as being a matter of course and to be expected. The Princess sensed this, and in an imperious tone of voice which called me "to order" she said: "I would have you remember these are *my* people."

During the early visits she impressed me with her sincerity of belief in spiritual powers and the continuity of life after the earthly phase had terminated. In her forthright way, she told me that death "is just like going from one room into another".

As the years passed by and her life advanced she suffered from tiredness, often due to her busy and exacting life; then she would come for what she termed "a fill-up" with vitality and strength. Three days before the Coronation of Her Majesty the Queen, she came for this purpose, explaining how very tiring some of the receptions were when she had to stand for a long time while guests were being presented to the Queen. She was very conscious on these occasions of being fortified with new strength and vitality.

One day she asked Mrs. Burton and I whether we would like a portrait of her. We said we would and in due course a photographic print arrived. On her next visit, she enquired if we had received her photograph, so we showed her the one which had been sent. She was indignant, for apparently it was a general print that was usually sent to the Press and to general enquirers, so she promised to send another. When this arrived it was a personally signed studio portrait of her in her coronation robes.

The following story was told to me by Her Royal Highness. One of her secretaries had been concerned about his wife who had had a stroke. He told the Princess that she had made a remarkable recovery and in a short time the effects of the stroke had disappeared. The secretary was a little apprehensive in telling her that he had written to a healer in Surrey for spiritual healing, but he firmly attributed his wife's speedy recovery to this. The Princess laughed as she told of her secretary's amazement when she said, "I know, you have been writing to Mr. Harry Edwards."

One day she purchased a copy of Mrs. Burton's book, *Spirit Stories for Children*. Some time afterwards she asked for another copy for, as she said, "a little boy, you know very well." She did not specifically say it was for H.R.H. Prince Charles, but the imputation was there.

In 1955, it was arranged for the Princess to undertake a sea voyage to South Africa for health reasons, but she was apprehensive as to whether she could do this and two days before she sailed she came to the Sanctuary to receive her "fill-up" of new strength. The voyage was successful, and as soon as she returned to this country she came to the Sanctuary to express her thanks.

Early in 1956, Princess Marie Louise contracted pneumonia and was seriously ill. I received a telegram from her requesting absent healing to help her recover, and one of her ladies-in-waiting also wrote and told me how the Princess was causing much concern by refusing to obey the doctor's instructions, not taking the medicines and drugs prescribed.

Dated by the day I received the telegram, a change for the better was observed and a rapid recovery followed which her doctors could not understand. She declared her faith in spiritual healing and was conscious of the help reaching her, and she shocked her doctors and friends by declaring she would be going to a Spring Charity Ball the following week. Her doctor remonstrated with her and said, "It would be madness," but she responded to the healing so quickly that she duly attended the Ball without any suggestion of a relapse. The Princess was then 84.

From this time onwards, she came to us for healing every few weeks, but it became obvious that age was taking its toll and her resistance weakening; but she was always better for her healing. From all the information I gathered, she would not let herself rest; her mind was so active and she continued to carry out her public duties without respite. When I told her how necessary it was to conserve her energies and take life more gently I knew she would not heed my advice. It was her selflessness in helping others and various good causes that played its part in sapping her strength in the latter days. She was truly a spiritual soul, natural and with little regard for convention, and one who lived for others.

Once she spoke to me about the attitude of the Church to healing. As she walked up and down the Sanctuary, she exclaimed: "I cannot understand it, the Church should be doing this work of healing and it is not. What can we do to wake the Church up, for did He not tell the Church to 'heal the sick'."

Princess Marie Louise was one of the five surviving grandchildren of Queen Victoria and of these five, four have received spiritual healing in the Sanctuary or by absent healing. The Queen of Spain was one of these.

A year before she died the Princess wrote a book of her memoirs, and its publication was to be launched at a Foyle's Luncheon. She came to Burrows Lea two days before the luncheon date. It was to be her last visit to us. She was very weak and frail, and needed to be assisted into the lounge by her lady-in-waiting and her chauffeur. When I went in, she apologised for not being able to go into the Sanctuary for she had not the strength to go those few extra yards. She told me about the book and her luncheon date, and asked if I could give her the strength to fulfil this last function. I am sure she was aware of the approaching end of her earthly life, for she told me she had no fear of passing on because she knew there was a life in spirit ahead of her—but she would just like to have sufficient strength to help her attend the launching of her book.

We did all we could, purposefully infusing strength into her, and when we had finished, she got up by herself and walked unaided to her car, exclaiming, "See! I can do this now."

She had her wish. She attended the luncheon and gave her full speech in response to the toast in her honour. A few days later she passed into spirit life.

I received an official invitation to be present at the funeral service in St. George's Chapel, Windsor, and perhaps this was the only occasion when a spiritual healer was to be invited to a Royal function. I had healing appointments arranged for that day and I felt that the Princess would far rather have me help the sick and not cancel the appointments, so I arranged for my Secretary,

Miss Phyllis Harding to go and represent the Sanctuary at the service.

Another member of the Royal Family it was my privilege to help, was the Duke of Athlone. Because other participants are still living, I am not able to relate the whole of this healing story, but these were the circumstances. The Duke was very ill with heart and internal trouble, and I was asked to direct absent healing to him. His response was so rapid that three days later he was out of danger. He felt so well that (as the story goes) he turned his doctors away.

The Duke was even at that time an elderly man but he lived for several more years. During these years I was kept informed about him, and those nearest to him expressed the very private view that he was maintained through spiritual healing. When his final illness came upon him, it was feared that he would suffer a stressful passing unless he was kept under sedation. I was kept informed by telephone about the Duke's condition and was told that he refused to take the drugs. As his life faded away it did so quite peacefully, with natural sleep and no need for sedation.

News of these healings of the Royal Family became known and strange stories appeared in the American and Continental Press that were quite untrue. For example, under the title heading of "Harry Edwards and the Queen of England" a German magazine called *Das Zeitalter*, printed a picture of Her Majesty the Queen and in the text underneath it, were words to the effect that the Queen had been influenced by me for many years and that I arranged for spiritual healing for her; further, that I had worked intimately with a Mr. Cyril Henry Dams (whom I had never even heard of) and that together we had given healing to the Queen. In the accompanying article, it went on to say that Harry Edwards had "healed the Queen's horses" and made other statements equally untrue. The article continued that officials at Buckingham Palace denied the facts in a way that suggested they were "covering up" for the Queen.

It was most regrettable that the good name of our beloved Queen should have been the subject of irresponsible foreign journalism and for my part I had the deepest regret that my name had been linked with that of Her Majesty and so used to cause her annoyance.

I am not at liberty to divulge the name of the person who brought two of the Royal Princesses of Greece to the Sanctuary one day to observe a healing session, but when it was over, their Royal Highnesses stayed behind and asked me if I could help them. One suffered from arthritis in the shoulder and arms, the other from migraine and nervous headaches. I gave them both treatment, and whilst I could not expect to hear from them personally as to how they were progressing, some time later the one who brought them to the Sanctuary told me they had both been free from their troubles ever since.

I will tell only one further story concerning the healing of an "important" person (although *all* people are surely important, especially if they are sick!). My part in this healing took place with the co-operation of the War Office and the Admiralty.

Soon after the Second World War ended, the Governor of Guernsey became seriously ill. His relatives were convinced that he could be helped through spiritual healing, and I was approached to see if I would be willing to go to Guernsey. I said I would, but travelling in those days was very much curtailed by regulations. However, the Governor's son was a staff officer at the War Office in London, and he was able to arrange for a special military charter flight to fly me to Guernsey and bring me back. With the son as my escort, we flew from Croydon, but unfortunately the plane could not land owing to weather conditions and we had to return to Croydon.

The following week I was on my annual holiday in Ventnor, on the Isle of Wight. There, I was contacted by a military representative and asked if I would consent to go and see if healing could help the Governor. I agreed, and was driven by the officer at speed over the island to Cowes to catch the ferry to Southampton, where a corvette had been detailed to take me to Guernsey. I recall how anxious the officer was about the time, for he feared we should be too late to catch the ferry. Half-way there, he stopped the car and telephoned to Cowes asking for the ferry to be held up until we arrived. We were only a few minutes late, but I remember motoring up to the ferry and seeing it crowded with people, staring at me in a none too friendly way as I hastened aboard. On reaching Southampton I was told what dock to go to and started to walk, looking out for that particular dock. I then had no idea of the extent of the dock area, but eventually I arrived, and once on board, the corvette immediately put to sea. I was very well looked after on the journey, which took all night and well into the morning of the following day. I well remember that turbulent voyage.

I was met on arrival and taken straight away to the Governor's residence, where I found him in great distress and very ill from cancer. His condition was far advanced and his doctors expected him to pass over any day.

As I held his hands and sought for help from Spirit to reach him, I was conscious of a sense of calmness coming to him and also with myself. Hitherto, owing to the pain, he had not slept for a long time, apart from the sleep induced through drugs, but as I held his hands he became peaceful and slept. I stayed at the Residency that night, and attended him again the next morning. He had slept peacefully right through the night, and there was a smile on his face as he thanked me for the "peace that had come to him". Later that day, I was flown back to Southampton to resume my vacation in the Isle of Wight.

The Governor lived for a while longer, but he was very weak for the disease had become very deep seated. He gradually faded away, but from the time I first saw him and held his hands, he suffered no more pain and needed no more drugs. He slept naturally and passed into his spirit life peacefully. The physicians told his wife that this was incomprehensible to them and contrary to all expectations. They could not account for such a peaceful change suddenly coming to him, and I remember a descriptive sentence in a letter I received from his wife afterwards in which she wrote: "It was as if an angel had spread his wings over him."

From a medical point of view, it might be thought that spiritual healing had failed, because a recovery did not take place; but in view of all the circumstances I think it was a spiritual healing just the same.

CHAPTER FIVE

HEALING WITH DOCTORS

SOME years ago, I was invited by a medical society to demonstrate spiritual healing to its members. The meeting took place in a large house near Harley Street, London. My colleagues and I were shown into a spacious room where some thirty doctors were seated on easy chairs and couches which had been carefully arranged round the walls and in the centre of the room were three wooden chairs for our use.

I had previously proposed that the doctors should bring their own patients, to avoid any possibility of collusion and because the doctors would be conversant with the diagnosis and medical histories of their patients.

We were not introduced personally, and there were no introductory speeches; the secretary of the society simply said that we had come to demonstrate spiritual healing and called for the first patient to be brought in. Thus it was in this cold and uncongenial atmosphere, a lady suffering from disseminated sclerosis was helped in, supported by two attendants. Her paralysis was far advanced for she could only slowly shuffle along dragging one foot up to the other.

She was seated with difficulty on one of the wooden chairs and supported by Mr. George Burton. I sat on one of the other chairs facing her. I soon discovered what I had expected to find, namely that she had a poker-back spine. I pointed this out to the assembly, but they did not seem interested. I was able to get the spine to palpate freely in a minute or so, so that she could bend her back forwards, backwards and sideways. I told the doctors what I had done, performing an act of healing which was impossible to medical practice. The doctors continued to be apathetic, uninterested and rather bored, and I could see that they were determined not to give me any encouragement, or to acknowledge any change for the better.

Through obtaining spinal mobility, the paralysing pressures on the nerves was removed, so then the next phase of the healing was to see to what extent the lady could use her legs. With gentle encouragement she was able to lift her knees reasonably by herself and to stretch out her legs in front of her. I also sought for the loosening of her ankles (which were tightly locked) and for control over the pointing of her feet.

The interest of the doctors became aroused when I asked her to stand up, which she was able to do fairly easily, and next, to lift each knee up as high as she could, which was also accomplished. When the doctors saw this, they realised that indeed something had happened that they could not account for. One doctor got up and came close, and before long all the others followed, and for the rest of the afternoon I had an uncomfortably close audience. They watched the lady walk out of the room haltingly, but reasonably well. An excited discussion followed in which I heard one rather distinguished-looking doctor describe the improvements as the result of "suggestion".

The second patient was a man in his thirties who was also a sufferer from the same disease. His feet were dragging and he had to be supported and helped in by two friends. With great difficulty he was placed on the chair, and needed Mr. Burton's constant support to prevent his falling off.

I turned to the doctor who had spoken about "suggestion", saying: "If you think spiritual healing is simply suggestion, here is a patient ready to receive all the suggestions you and your friends can make to him. See what you can do." My offer was not taken up. I further said, "Isn't this man deemed to be totally incurable and incapable of receiving benefit?" to which the doctors readily assented.

The healing procedure was similar to that of the previous patient, and after about ten minutes the man was able, with my holding his hands, to stand up on his legs for a time before they gave way. The standing and sitting down process was repeated. Then after a short rest, I got the man to stand up again and raise each foot off the floor and make a short step, and from thence to walk a little way, supported on either side by his friends. The

HEALING WITH DOCTORS

patient and his friends were overjoyed and the doctors were deeply impressed.

Patient followed patient, there was one suffering from paralysis following stroke, two others crippled with rheumatoid arthritis. Each of them responded to an appreciable degree, one of the arthritic cases being able to lift his hands above his head and to walk without his two sticks.

So the afternoon went on, until it finally ended up with the doctors themselves asking for treatment for their own troubles! One might have thought that these doctors would have been sufficiently interested to wish to carry on further investigation, but I heard no further from them.

It is not an uncommon thing for doctors to bring their patients or relatives to the Sanctuary for healing, or to request it for themselves. All this needs to be carried out in strict confidence, for if it was known that these doctors were "associating" with me, they would become liable for disciplinary action by the British Medical Council. Indeed, after a statement on spiritual healing in the *British Medical Journal* this threat was repeated. I recall the case of the doctor who assisted Sir Herbert Barker, being struck off the register for the same "crime". Therefore, in the cases that follow, the names of the doctors cannot be mentioned, unless they have passed on from earthly life or have since retired.

I can, however, mention Dr. W. P. Over, Physician and Surgeon, who during his active medical life, frequently introduced or brought patients to the Sanctuary for healing. One day he came, unexpectedly, doubled over with pain from a slipped disc. He said: "They want me to go into hospital for treatment and I know what that means. Can you help me?"

I sat him down before me, and with one hand on his right shoulder and the other on the lumbar region of the spine, I could feel the anger of pain in his back and also "see" where the offending cartilage was exerting pressure on the nerves emerging from the spinal column. With a few gentle movements to express the healing intention, the vertebrae moved naturally and as easily as they should and the cartilage was restored to its correct position. The healing took about three minutes and after this Dr. Over was able to stand upright and flex his back freely without even a twinge of pain. He never forgot this demonstration of the art of spiritual healing, and in his later years he wrote a book *It Was Revealed Unto Me*, in which many spiritual experiences including healing, are related.

An ever-increasing number of doctors, in their private capacity are co-operating with spiritual healing, and even the hospitals are more free in sending their special patients for treatment, providing an ambulance to carry the patient to and from the Sanctuary with nurses in attendance.

I remember an occasion when I was asked to address a Division of the British Medical Association. The meeting was held in the house of one of the doctors. When we arrived we found about twenty doctors assembled, and not knowing what kind of reception I was going to get, I felt a little apprehensive. I had no need to worry, for the doctors were very pleasant and friendly. It was hardly a sedate gathering for they were seated round the room drinking, with spare bottles of beer under their chairs.

I spoke on spiritual healing without pulling any punches and afterwards answered their questions. Some of which were critical, others searching. When the meeting was over, the company moved into an adjacent room for refreshments and Irish coffee. As we were about to leave the room, a doctor button-holed me and whispered in a conspiratorial manner: "I'm your best friend here." I acknowledged this gladly. On moving out into the passage, another doctor coming down the stairs called me aside and said words to the same effect. When we were leaving and had settled into the car, I saw another doctor hurrying down the path, holding his hand up in a delaying gesture. I wound down the window. The doctor came up and assured me, in confidence, that he believed in our work, and he was our greatest supporter in the district. The importance of this was, that while the doctors were on the most cordial and friendly terms with their fellows, calling them by their Christian and nick-names, they did not wish their contemporaries to know that they were in favour of spiritual healing.

A doctor consulted me about his teen-age son. The lad was mentally retarded, obstinate, irresponsible, resisted parental control, had fits and was violent towards his mother and sister, took no interest in his schooling and refused to co-operate with medical treatment. The parents were in despair. The one thing the lad liked and excelled in was sport.

The doctor told me he had taken his son to medical specialists, to psychiatrists, neurologists and so on. They declared there was nothing they could do for him. It was a case of incurability, linked up with a brain disease which caused his fits. The father was advised that it was dangerous for his son to be either at school or at home, for there was no knowing what he might do. It was finally recommended that he should arrange for a constant guard companion to be with his son at all times or else to commit him to institutional care.

The father was reluctant to take these steps and asked me if I would see his son, but he knew that any direct approach would be resisted, so the visit was arranged for, by subterfuge. It was agreed that when the doctor was driving his son back to school he would make a diversion to call at the Sanctuary on the pretext of looking at the garden. He did this, and his son accompanied him into the gardens, where "by chance" I met them.

I commenced chatting to the boy on ordinary things, the fish in the pond, the flowers and the view and we slowly drew away from the father. I enquired where he was going and was told he was going back to school, which he did not like. I sympathised with him. I could see that the lad valued an opportunity to talk and express himself freely to someone who was not a relative. It seemed as if a bond of friendship was established between us and I had achieved an "entry" into his mind. We undertook to write to each other.

The lad wrote to me occasionally to which I replied, encouraging his confidence. The father also kept me closely informed about his son, while I maintained absent healing for him.

From the day we talked in the garden the lad had no more fits. He was more attentive to some of his studies, and the school reports indicated a measureable improvement, but when he went home on holiday, he still occasionally showed the worst side of his character to his parents and sister.

Naturally, a healing of this nature was progressive and through the good influencing from spirit the lad gradually became more receptive, developing a more normal outlook. The healing continued for him for several years. He improved so much with his studies that he was able to enter a university; he continued to excel in sport and rowed in the University boat races. As time went on so his healing brought about a complete change for the good, in all ways. He appreciated his home, his father became a companion, he revered his mother and championed his younger sister. When he left the University he was employed as a representative by one of the best-known firms in Britain.

His father, the doctor, became an enthusiastic supporter of spiritual healing and would write to me for himself and his wife, as well as for those of his patients for whom he thought spiritual healing would be beneficial.

We have treated many similar cases and, generally, allowing for a few exceptions where the parents did not continue to keep in touch with us, we have been told of the transformations which have taken place in establishing an orderly outlook, good conduct and the awakening of perspective and awareness of life's responsibilities. Such healings take time to bring about, being, as it were, a contest between the healing purpose and the patient's repressed nature. The satisfactory outcome can only be accounted for by continual good influencing reaching the patient's spirit self and so arousing a sense of good conscience and purpose.

A very well-known lady doctor, who at one time was constantly appearing on television consulted me about a lad similarly affected as in the case related. Again we were happy to see satisfactory results.

One doctor whose name I can give now that she has passed on into the higher life, was Doctor M. Vivian. This doctor was a physician whose practice was in Southbourne, Bournemouth, and was also consulting physician to the Marley Nursing Home. Dr. Vivian was a believer in spiritual healing and would send to me special patients thought to be "incurable" and for whom no medical treatment would be of no avail. The four cases that follow are described in the doctor's own words.

"*Case 1.* Three years ago the patient contracted a skin disease known as Sycosis Barbae, an intractable and very distressing complaint. For reasons connected with the war, it was the better part of a year before he could obtain expert treatment, and the specialists then informed him that, owing to the delay, the prospects of a cure were remote. I mentioned the case to a colleague,

HEALING WITH DOCTORS 49

who replied, 'Having had no treatment for nine months, he will be fortunate if he is cured in nine years.'

"For nearly two years he attended the skin departments of various hospitals in London and in the provinces, and though a temporary improvement was occasionally observed, the sores on his face did not heal and the area they covered slowly increased.

"Last April, Edwards was asked to treat the case, and when I saw the patient about a fortnight ago, his face had entirely healed, nothing remaining but the pale scars showing where the sores had been. As in other cases I have seen treated by Edwards the cure was gradual, only a slight improvement being observed during the first few weeks. Then suddenly the healing process accelerated until the sores disappeared."

"*Case 2*. This was a woman complaining of progressive loss of weight, intolerable fatigue and a steady deterioration in health for which her doctor could find no adequate cause. He attributed it to anxieties and malnutrition connected with the war and prescribed the usual remedies. Things, however, went from bad to worse, until she could scarcely walk and found it difficult to force herself to eat.

"In the late Autumn, Edwards was approached and commenced treatment. For some weeks there was no particular improvement, but suddenly, on the morning of Christmas Day, the patient felt better and to her friends' surprise ate a large dinner of turkey and plum pudding. From that day, she improved steadily and today is in excellent health, and has regained the two stones in weight lost during her illness.

"I do not know what caused the trouble, but it can have had nothing to do with war conditions since these were unchanged during the period of cure."

"*Case 3*. This patient suffered from an intractable varicose ulcer on the skin, complicated by varicose veins of long standing. As it did not respond to treatment, Edwards's help was invoked, without any great hope of success on account of the time the trouble had been in existence. For some time nothing much happened. It did not spread, but showed little signs of healing, probably because the patient was unable to rest the limb.

"Then, suddenly, about a fortnight ago, it began to heal rapidly. The swelling subsided, and today the sore is less than half its original size, and if progress is maintained at the same rate, it should be entirely healed within the next fortnight. Varicose ulcers, as all doctors know, seldom heal unless rest in bed can be obtained."

"*Case 4*. This is another case of long outstanding varicose veins. Both legs were much swollen, and the least abrasion threatened an indolent ulcer similar to that of Case 3. The patient is a very busy woman, and in wartime was scarcely off her feet.

"In spite of this, the swelling has subsided since Edwards started treating her, and she says, she feels ten years younger.

"It will be noted that all these cases were most unpromising from the medical point of view. Not one of them has ever met Edwards, who gave them what is known as absent treatment. I have no notion how the treatment works; all I can say is that the conditions were as stated."

Dr. Vivian specially wrote these descriptions for a book published in 1953, *Harry Edwards and His Healing* by Maurice Barbanell (now out of print).

After this, Dr. Vivian supervised a special kind of nursing home for the treatment of drug addiction. When there was a particularly chronic case, that showed reluctance to respond to medical treatment, Dr. Vivian would write to me for absent healing for the patient. In the majority of cases, the patients began to respond to treatment as soon as absent healing intercession commenced. This doctor continued to seek the aid of spiritual healing for all the difficult conditions until retirement.

Doctors in some Continental countries, particularly in Germany and Holland take a more objective view of healing than those in the United Kingdom. When we have demonstrated healing in Holland at large gatherings, a number of doctors secured the front platform seats, and during the demonstration became a nuisance at times by crowding round us and the patient to watch the good changes take place, but unfortunately obscuring the view of the audience.

Since the publication of some of my books into the German language, a considerable number of professors and doctors have written to me for absent healing for other doctors, relatives, friends and patients. These German doctors are meticulous in regularly reporting progress and, as success is seen, so they add to their list of people for whom they seek help.

An amusing incident occurred when we held a healing service in the very large Concert Hall in Haarlem, Holland. In all Continental countries spiritual contact healing is forbidden by law. For example, in Holland, no one can be admitted to a healing meeting unless he becomes a member of the society, and even then records in quintuplicate have to be made for each person attending. The magnitude of this task can be imagined, when the very largest halls needed to be booked to accommodate the two, three or four thousand people who desired to be present.

At the Haarlem meeting, the official part of the service had ended, but hundreds of sick people remained behind to receive treatment and we were kept busy for some hours afterwards. As midnight approached an excited messenger reported to the organisers (our mutual friends and fellow healers, Mr. and Mrs. Ph. van Gunckel), that a posse of police had entered the hall. There was consternation. All the remaining people were hurried out of the hall through a side exit, and we made our way towards the main entrance where we saw half a dozen, black uniformed, jack-booted armed police. Mr. and Mrs. Gunckel were perturbed for they thought we might all be arrested. But there was no need for alarm for the corporal in charge of the police came up to us, and asked if we would heal the rheumatism in his leg—which we most gladly did.

CHAPTER SIX

HEALING IN CYPRUS

IN 1954, Mr. and Mrs. Burton and I accepted an invitation to conduct a healing mission in Cyprus. There were to be two healing demonstrations in the cinema in Nicosia. Mr. Burton would return on the third day to England to carry on the healing work at the Sanctuary, while Mrs. Burton and I were to remain for the rest of the week, with the intention of having a rest.

On our arrival at the airport, a gathering of the island's notable people were there to greet us, and gave us large bunches of flowers. Later, George Burton commented that he felt like a "ninny" carrying his flowers.

We stayed at the Ledra Palace Hotel in Nicosia, but from the moment we arrived until Mrs. Burton and I "escaped" (I use the word in its fullest sense) from the island we were besieged by the sick every hour of the day.

We had a suite of rooms with a salon, or lounge, in the centre. Each morning, even before we got up, the hotel corridors were teeming with sick and crippled people. In their eagerness they did not hesitate to invade our rooms, and the mornings were continuously devoted to healing the sick. After one heavy morning the number of applicants had diminished and towards noon the end was in sight. Almost the last patient was a uniformed inspector of police troubled with arthritic hips. He responded very well to the healing and could soon move his legs freely without any pain. A few minutes after he left we were somewhat dismayed to find yet another crowd of people arriving. Apparently the inspector was so overjoyed with the relief the healing had given to him, he had run out into the main street, shouting at the top of his voice about his cure and urging all who were sick to go straight away to the Ledra Palace to get healing!

HEALING IN CYPRUS

The organisers, a Mr. Andreas and his friends, did their best to keep our visit "organised" but quickly found themselves helpless against the numbers of people who crowded for healing on every occasion. We were taken on a trip to see the Cypriot Governor of Nicosia in his palace, but even there a healing session took place. We said we would like to see the Port of Famagusta, so our friends arranged for cars and one afternoon we set off to see the city. On the way we glimpsed the famous Othello Tower out of the car window. We were taken to a restaurant for tea where some two hundred people had been assembled to take tea with us. Then, came the apparently innocent question, "Would we like to visit a medical establishment?" and, unsuspectingly, we said we would. It was not far to walk, and on arrival we discovered that the "medical establishment" was a doctor's surgery, where it appeared to me from the paraphernalia there and various notices hanging on the walls, the doctor's principle vocation was the treatment of venereal disease. The doctor asked if we would see one of his patients and we could not refuse; but instead of just one patient it became a procession, which went on so long that at last we had to say: "No more." When we emerged from the doctor's surgery, it was quite dark, and so apart from the Othello Tower, that was all we saw of Famagusta.

The next day, as a "rest day", we were taken to visit Kyrenia. Our hosts promised there would be no healing. We were to have lunch at the house of an editor of one of the Cyprus newspapers. As we were approaching the house, our cars were stopped by a messenger frantically waving his arms. He gave us the news that our visit had become known and the editor's house was besieged by a crowd of sufferers seeking healing, so we were diverted to the house of another friend. It was no use, for the news got around as to where we were, and before we knew it, the sick came flocking in and once again Mrs. Burton and I settled down to an exhausting healing session that went on and on, until finally Mrs. Burton put her foot down and said: "No more."

On our way back to Nicosia, we stopped at a friend's house for tea, with the same result—another healing session!

The man of the house, asked us if we could help him, and this is a healing case worth recalling. He had a physical disability that prevented him from fathering children, and his wife had become neurotic for she wanted children very much. The husband had visited specialists in America, Switzerland and in Great Britain and had been told by all the specialists, who were in agreement, that the cause of his infertility was incurable and no medical treatment would be of any avail. Nevertheless, we sought for healing to be with him, hoping that it might be within the scheme of things for his weakness to be overcome. Some years later, I met this man and his wife again and was delighted to learn they had two children.

Before I relate what happened at the two fantastic healing demonstrations, I must tell of another experience at this time. Our aeroplane stopped at Athens for a while, and all the passengers had to disembark. When we entered the departure lounge, we found people and Press photographers awaiting us. Apparently our Cyprus friends in their eagerness had telegraphed the information about our movements ahead of us. Mrs. Burton was presented with two Greek dolls in national costume. The photographers flashed their bulbs, the reporters asked questions and an officer asked for healing. We did not refuse, and so we had the unique experience of holding a healing session before a crowd of people in the Athens Airport lounge. All the other passengers had gone aboard the plane but we were still carrying on with the healing when a stewardess came and told us the plane was waiting.

The two public healing demonstrations in Cyprus remain my most poignant memory. They took place in a large cinema in the centre of Nicosia and, when we arrived, the wide roadway in front of the cinema was a chaotic mass of people, motor-cars, horse carts, and vehicles of all kinds, all in a turbulent mass of movement. A way was made for us to get inside.

The cinema accommodated over a thousand people and it was packed to capacity. The noise was terrific, with the people shouting one to the other, reaching a crescendo like a "sea of noise". There were vendors of food and drink and sales were booming. I could not tell what they were selling but it looked like bottles of beer and the equivalent of our "hot dogs". A more irreverent and unspiritual gathering it would be hard to imagine.

The meeting commenced with addresses in Greek and Turkish, by the chairman and a Greek medical Professor from Athens, the latter possessing a powerful voice rivalling that of a Guards' sergeant-major. With his harsh and strident voice he went on and on with vigour, haranguing and, it would seem, severely admonishing the audience, but I think he was simply trying to get the audience quiet. Certainly it was hushed when Mrs. Burton gave the prayer of invocation.

All my comments had to be translated by an interpreter into Greek and Turkish, so the progress of the demonstration was slowed right down. For a while we had reasonable order and the cases of infirmity which came up on to the platform responded wonderfully well. I remember the case of a spastic child who had never walked, making his first steps on the platform. I cannot now recall all the detail of those healings, but perhaps the finest tribute which could be paid, was that for the first half an hour the audience were quiet and attentive. But as the time went on, and the sick people and their relatives realised the number we could treat was limited the audience grew restless. At times, the stentorian voice of the Greek professor was called upon to restore some semblance of order.

The platform was about five feet high and had no railing in front. A treatment was being given when one man, bold enough to defy convention, strode down one of the gangways carrying in his arms a crippled body without any limbs, and pushed it on to the platform at our feet. This was the signal for others to do the same, and in a minute or two the platform was laden with the bodies of men, women and children, many of whom were crippled or sick from one illness or another. It was heart-rending—a terrible scene as more and more sufferers were coming forward, seemingly without end.

We were helpless against this human tidal wave and could do nothing else but leave the platform and so close the meeting.

The second demonstration took place the following night. Once again pandemonium reigned outside the cinema, for thousands could not get in, and inside the place was packed.

I asked the Greek professor to explain to the people what had happened the previous night when we had to leave the platform, and if we were to carry on that evening it must be orderly. The professor did his best. What he said I do not know, but judging from the intensity of his loud voice and the long duration of his comments, he succeeded in impressing the audience for they became quiet and even the vendors of beer were quiet.

For a short time the healing was allowed to proceed in a reasonably orderly manner, with the interpreters explaining what was taking place until, I remember, the bent-over body of a cripple became straight and upright.

The effect of this on the audience was amazing! People stood up and shouted acclamation, and then reserve broke down and there came a repetition of the previous night, only this time they were not content with depositing their sick ones on the platform, but almost invaded it, shouting to us imploringly to heal their particular dear one.

It became impossible to carry on as the whole mass of the audience were on their feet pushing their way on to the platform. The organisers enclosed us and slowly we had to force our way through the throng to the back of the platform where a wooden stairway ascended to the manager's office. We managed to get up the stairs safely and together and, once inside, the door was shut. Down below the people waited and it looked as if we would be marooned in the little upper office for some time. The people with their sick ones would not go away, and were determined to wait until we had seen them.

After a while, the police came and took command of the stairway, but all was not yet over, for the police then brought *their own* relatives up the stairs for healing. Thus, the healing service was transferred from the cinema hall to the little office, the police bringing in their people, one at a time, for there was no room for more than one.

So we stayed there healing, until the night was far gone. At last, we were able to return to the hotel for a few hours' sleep before the final invasion of the sick ones in the early morning.

Our visit to Cyprus was hectic from the hour we arrived to the hour we, rather thankfully, boarded the aircraft for our departure.

CHAPTER SEVEN

CLASH WITH A SURGEON

PHILIP was a little boy of four. When one year old he contracted infantile paralysis and shortly before I saw him he had been discharged from hospital as "incurable", with one leg paralysed and useless so that he had to be kept in bed. Before he left the hospital, arrangements had been made for a full-length caliper with no knee joint to be made, and this was fitted only two weeks before his mother brought him to a healing service we were giving in Cambridge. With the aid of the caliper he could just manage to get about with much difficulty, dragging his leg behind him. His foot was badly twisted, too, which did not make standing on the weak leg any easier. When the caliper was taken off he could not walk even one step because the knee would give way and the leg was too weak to support the weight of his body.

This was Philip's condition when his mother carried him up the steps of the platform. I first sought for mobility and strength to reach his spine, then for co-ordination and vitality to be with the leg. I was then impressed to ask the mother to remove the caliper, which she did. I lifted the leg upwards at the hip to effect free movement, then placing the leg on mine, I asked the boy to lift the knee and depress it, and this he could do. I was conscious of strength returning to the movements. Again I asked the boy to lift the knee and I sought adjustment for the foot, and placing this against my body, I asked Philip to push me—which he was able to do with some strength. I was confident then, that the healing had taken place.

I told the boy to stand up and then raise each knee in turn and he could do this, without the paralysed leg giving way. Next, a few steps were tried and the boy could walk for the first time in his life. He walked as naturally as if he had been doing so for a long time and it was seen that the twisted foot was twisted no longer and was being used normally. He walked down the steps from the platform and for the remainder of the service he romped about in the space between the platform and the audience. He made so much noise doing this, that the mother took off his boots, and Philip continued to run about in his socks.

When the orthopaedic surgeon heard of this, he became angry and told the mother to put on the caliper. Philip had not been wearing this since his healing for he was walking and running about quite normally. The mother did not do what the surgeon told her.

At the same healing service, Philip's eleven-year-old sister, Thelma, was treated for the same disease. She had the complication of a spinal curvature which tilted her pelvis, and she wore a caliper, too. Under the healing I was able to bring about the realignment of the spine and the pelvic tilt disappeared. Her legs received strength, and she could walk fairly normally for the first time in her life without any aid. She had had a built-up boot to compensate for the shortening of the leg owing to the pelvic tilt, but when both her boots were removed it was seen that she could stand level and walk without any limp.

The local paper *The Peterborough Citizen and Advertiser* reported these healings in detail, as I have described them, and followed this up with an interview with the orthopaedic surgeon who had had the two children under his care and treatment. He then made the remarkable statement that the healing had had no beneficial effect.

The surgeon was reported to have said, "The treatment of infantile paralysis is an exact treatment, any variation from which could cause permanent paralysis in a person who otherwise would have got better. Therefore, as orthopaedic surgeon for Peterborough and district, I feel it is my duty to point out most strongly that, to the medical profession, there is only one treatment of infantile paralysis and that is on scientific and proved lines."

Questioned about Thelma, the surgeon said, "The tapping back of displaced bones in the spine is an age-old chiropractic stunt for which there is absolutely no medical foundation. If a person does displace one of the bones of the spine, it is an extremely serious injury and it most certainly requires more than a mild pushing back." He added, "Many psychic healers had such strong personalities that they could convince patients they were better even if they were not."

I replied to this newspaper comment and in this I said: "The surgeon does not question that the displaced vertebrae in Thelma's spine are now in place. She had this disability since birth. Her spine was corrected in a matter of seconds, with her body fully clothed and without even a twinge of pain.

"He is in obvious error when he assumes that the vertebrae were replaced by 'tapping' or 'chiropractic'. Such treatment would not be possible with a fully clothed body in the space of five seconds.

"The pertinent question is: Was not Thelma's case considered to be 'incurable'? If her spine could have been straightened by any process known to medical science, why was it not done? Thelma's improved walking was obvious to all.

"Concerning Philip, he was sent home incurable and no further treatment could be given apart from the caliper. He had to be carried up on to the platform. He had no strength at all in his paralysed leg which would give way and collapse under the slightest pressure. He could not support his body on his bad leg. After I had treated him, he walked down the stairs holding my fingers. The twist in his foot had disappeared. For the next hour he romped about the hall, without the caliper. His mother took his boots off to save him making so much noise.

"He (the surgeon) then suggests it was my strong personality that accomplished these things. Is such a theory tenable with a girl crippled from birth and a boy of only four years of age?

"Incidentally there was another lady (an adult) also suffering from the same complaint from birth, who was so helped that she could lift both legs knee-high and descended the stairs in a fairly normal fashion for the first time in her life. How can any influence of a mind over another's paralysed body of so long standing restore strength to paralysed limbs?

Some time later Philip's mother wrote to *Psychic News*.

"I, Mary Goodliffe, the mother of Philip Goodliffe, declare that Philip was born on June 4th, 1943. The trouble with his leg began about the end of August in the same year. He was taken to Peterborough Hospital as a suspect for infantile paralysis. This was later confirmed by the hospital at Newmarket. He could not use his leg at all.

"The iron was put on his leg about a week before he went to see Mr. Harry Edwards for treatment at Cambridge. After treatment by Mr. Edwards, the condition was very much better. He could run about without the iron.

"The surgeon had advised that he should continue to wear the iron, as this may help to strengthen the leg. Mr. Edwards did not suggest giving up the use of the iron immediately, but said he would probably want to use it occasionally and that he would need further treatment, the nature of which was indicated to the healers present.

"I have been advised by the doctors to give him as much rest as possible, but I find the greatest difficulty in doing this, as he is never still if he can possibly help it. He is full of life enjoying himself in every way like any normal child."

It is a pity, that when medical men are faced with the definite evidence of a super-normal healing, they are not prepared to believe the evidence before their eyes, evading this by such excuses that healers possess a wonder power of suggestion. The obvious reply to this is, "Why have not the doctors used their powers of persuasion over the years the patients have been in their care?"

I am reminded of another case when a similar excuse was given. A registered blind woman had not been able to see for forty years. She was brought to the Sanctuary, when Mrs. Burton placed her hands over the woman's eyes, seeking the spirit influences to restore the sight. When the hands were taken away, the woman could see. This case was referred to a doctor who was investigating spiritual healing privately, and in his report which was published in the *British Medical Journal*, the explanation of the restoration of the vision was attributed to our suggesting the woman could see and she could.

If this was the reason why the sight was restored, then one naturally asks, why was it, when the patient was an inmate of the eye hospital, the doctors had not made a similar suggestion. Can one imagine that any person who had become blind would not seek for themselves the return of their sight?

I know only too well the power of habit, but it takes excuses into the realm of absurdity to say that all a healer needs to do is to suggest to someone who has been blind for forty years that she can see—and she then can.

Here is the view of another surgeon. At a Coventry healing service a local surgeon·was invited to come on to the platform to watch and check patients' conditions before and after treatment. In a newspaper interview he stated: "There was a great improvement in the spinal cases which I examined. There is no doubt that the misalignments were reduced appreciably. Some of the cases of paralysis were of long standing, but there was an improvement. I do not know of any other form of treatment which would produce results so quickly."

CHAPTER EIGHT

THE HEALING OF ANIMALS

MOST healers who can relieve human suffering find that animals respond in the same way. Some healers are more successful with animals than with humans, and there is good reason for this. Let us see why.

Just as some people possess "green fingers" so others have the gift of being more akin to our lesser brethren than others. This kinship is mutual, for creatures, both winged and legged, take to some people more than they do to others.

I knew a man who could approach bad tempered bulls as if they were placid cows, whereas others had to use appliances to ensure their safety. This man tamed foxes and kept them in his garden, playing with them as if they were puppies. Horses would come and nuzzle him if he called or beckoned them.

I envied the man I once saw in Hyde Park who played with the sparrows as he fed them with crumbs of bread. He could get them to dance as they flew to catch the crumbs he threw into the air and to perch on his hand to take the food from his fingers. It was one of the happiest moments of my life, when seated in some public gardens, the sparrows came and took crumbs from my fingers.

I am sure that animals who are injured or sick know when they are in the presence of a healer. They give themselves into his care. Even dogs of the suspicious and temperamental kind who bark and snap at strangers, docilely permit a healer to handle them. I have never heard of an animal healer being scratched or bitten, even though the creature being attended was in pain.

I have not done a great deal of animal healing, but when there has been occasion to do so, happy results have invariably followed.

I recall the case of healing—of all things—a herd of cows. The

THE HEALING OF ANIMALS

farmer came to see me to ask for help. He was an understanding man, of good nature, and from his personal experiences had good reason to believe in the efficacy of healing.

He told me his herd of cows was very sick. The veterinary surgeon had just examined them and had diagnosed the entire herd to be suffering from chronic streptococci mastitis. This diagnosis was so serious that it could mean the herd would never again be useful for milk production and might even have to be destroyed. So it was that the farmer whose herd was situated at Newlands Corner, a Surrey beauty spot not far from the Sanctuary, came at once to enlist the aid of spiritual healing.

I told the farmer that as soon as he left I would enter into intercession to seek healing for the cows and, for his part he should return right away and gently massage their udders with his hands, having at the same time thoughts in his mind that the mastitis would yield and go.

The farmer did this and, while it may be hard for a sceptic to believe, the morning after he found all the udders soft and by the end of the day all symptoms of hardness and soreness had disappeared.

I understand that in normal circumstances when a cow has mastitis of one or more quarters it takes some days of careful nursing, with injections, before it gets well and even then the quarters may not yield any milk, or at best, a reduced quantity. In the case of the herd in question the milk yield began to return the day after the healing and this increased to normal one day later.

When the veterinary surgeon called on the morning following the healing, he was astonished. The farmer reported to me that he had exclaimed, "What is the matter with me; have I been dreaming?" He again visited the farm with even more astonishment when he found the udders functioning so well and the milk yield so good. "Who can explain miracles?" he said. He asked the farmer how he accounted for the phenomenal recovery, and what treatment he had given to his herd. The farmer replied "just spiritual healing" which the veterinary surgeon thought was a great joke.

A lady had a brown poodle dog, the largest poodle I had ever seen. It had developed a growth as big as a grapefruit in the lower chest, between the forelegs, with the result that its health had declined and a marked lassitude had set in. This dog was dearly loved by all the family and they brought him to me several times for treatment. On each occasion the size of the growth diminished, and from a very hard texture it became soft and pulpy. The dog's health condition improved very much, for he was now eating well and keeping active. Clearly the trouble was being dispersed. The owners of the poodle were then advised by a veterinary surgeon to take the dog to a medical institution in Oxford for specialised treatment which I understood to be radium therapy. While undergoing this treatment the dog died. I often wondered if the spiritual healing process was negatived by the deep ray therapy enlivening the condition and so causing the death.

Apart from animals, I have known a number of cases of people suffering from "incurable" diseases, like growths, Addison's disease, etc., who were responding excellently under spiritual healing as far as I could judge from the disappearance of the pain and swellings, coupled with improvement in the general health tone. They would continue to make good progress until they were given deep ray therapy; then, from the commencement of the ray treatment deterioration would be observed sometimes with fatal results.

There was a wonderful talking budgerigar in Southampton. His name was Tony. His vocabulary was extensive and he had auditions at the B.B.C. This budgie became ill, he lost his feathers, moped, and looked a very poor specimen indeed. The owner was very distressed and wrote for absent healing for her pet and taught him to say, "Harry Edwards heal me". The bird soon recovered and grew a brighter dress of plumage than before. This bird was indeed receptive to healing for each time he showed signs of sickness, I would be told of this so that absent healing could be extended to him, and always he seemed to respond at once. Tony lived to a very old age before he flew into spirit life.

The following story is a favourite of mine. One day a van drew up in the forecourt of Burrows Lea. A man and his wife had brought a very sick Alsatian dog. They opened the doors of the van and I went in. The dog was lying on blankets, and as I looked at it, it seemed very near to death. The body was wasted and very thin, the hind part of the body and legs were paralysed, and the dog's eyes were sunken and glazed over. I sat down by the dog for a while and held its head in my hands as I sought for healing to help it in all ways that was still possible. There seemed to be no response and after a while, I laid the dog's head gently down and took the owners into the house, where we had a cup of tea together.

I told them I thought their dog was dying. We talked for about half an hour, when they got up to take their leave. I said to them: "Let us just take another look at your dog."

When the rear van doors were opened our astonishment was great, for there stood the dog, standing up on his four legs and wagging his tail! He joyously came towards us, but did not go to his master or mistress, coming straight to me, to be fondled as if he knew quite well that he had to express his gratitude. We gave the dog some milk and food which pleased my visitors for he had not been able to take any nourishment for some time.

These instances of animal healing can be multiplied many times over from the records of animal healers. Because animals respond in the same way to spiritual healing as people do, they must be in harmony with Spirit in order to be able to receive healing from that source. The implications arising from this are important, for they lead to the conclusion that animals possess souls and there is an after-life for them in Spirit when their earthly phase of life has ended.

CHAPTER NINE

AN EXPERIMENT IN MASS HEALING

SOME years ago the whole world was smitten with a disease which started in the Far East and which spread progressively to all other countries. It was the notorious "Asian 'flu" epidemic. The death roll from it was considerable, and as it was possible to judge the speed with which the epidemic progressed from country to country, so the time was accurately calculated when it would reach the United Kingdom, the people being warned accordingly.

From this advance notice we were able to institute a healing experiment. As the time drew nearer for the infection to reach these shores we published in *The Spiritual Healer* an invitation for our readers to join in this experiment. In addition, we enclosed in some twenty thousand letters sent out to the many who were at that time receiving absent healing a notice to the same effect.

The notice said that we would be holding a mass absent healing intercession for all our patients and readers in order that they might be protected from the disease. We asked our patients and readers to inform us at once if they caught Asian 'flu, or had its symptoms. It is estimated that forty thousand people were covered in this experiment.

The epidemic reached Britain at the time expected, and it hit the population very hard indeed, especially in the Midlands and in the North. Factories had to close down. Most families had victims from the scourge. Schools had to be closed because so many children were ill. Many people died.

The result of our experiment was surprising. The number of letters we received telling us that our readers, patients and their families had been infected was very few indeed—about a score. Considering the number of people involved in the experiment and that many of them lived in badly infected areas, by all normal reckoning we should have received reports of from 500 to a 1,000 infected cases.

One school head mistress wrote to ask if we would place her school children within the protective influencing of spiritual healing and this request was given special thought in our absent healing intercessions. The result was, that while every other school in the area had to close down, this particular school had no need to, for the number of children who became ill was surprisingly few, and even those were very mild cases.

I can also mention that none of our staff contracted Asian 'flu.

It is not the purpose of this book to go deeply into the ways and means by which healings take place, its purpose being to record facts relating to successful healing results; nevertheless, the implications arising from this successful experiment are significant.

In my previous book *The Healing Intelligence*, the PROTECTIVE potential in spiritual healing is dealt with at length, for it is a logical, but unprovable, statement, that many of our patients have been protected from contracting disease, particularly cancer, because of the ability of the healing influences to overcome the psychosomatic cause—the primary origin of so many of our diseases—and so enable the body to resist infection.

CHAPTER TEN

MIRACLE IN SURREY*

ALTHOUGH Bunyan's hero had so much in common with ourselves, although he shared so many of our doubts and faced so many of our dangers, it would be straining the analogy to suggest that at all times we can predict how he would have reacted to all the problems which confront our generation. In the whole of *Pilgrim's Progress* there is no territory in any way comparable to that which we are about to explore.

Not that it is wild or remote—in a geographical sense; it is merely a quiet lane near the village of Shere in Surrey. But we must not be deceived by the undramatic quality of the background. For in this lane there is a house of magic. It is called the Sanctuary; it is the headquarters of Harry Edwards, the spiritual healer; and we are going to visit it together, without any preliminaries and without any previous "briefing" or study of the evidence. Although we have made an appointment—for appointments are necessary—you do not really need one in order that Mr. Edwards may be able to turn on his magic. It is flowing all the time, night and day.

So here we are, walking down a long drive fringed with rhododendrons, crossing a courtyard (which already contains several cars from which cripples are painfully hobbling) ringing the front-door bell and being shown into a white room where some twenty patients are sitting in silence, waiting for the healer. And although we will assume that Christian is still with us, we will not venture to analyse his emotions.

*"Miracle in Surrey" is a chapter taken from Mr. Beverley Nichols's book *A Pilgrim's Progress*. Our thanks are due to the Publishers, Jonathan Cape Ltd., London, W.C.1, for permission to print this chapter.

It is a simple room, half-way between a doctor's consulting-room and a private chapel. Two or three rows of chairs are drawn up to face a long oak table, on which there stands a symbolic image made of perspex from the cockpit of a Stirling bomber—a cross surmounted by a circle. This is described by Mr. Edwards as "a modern version of converting the sword into a ploughshare". On the walls hang three pictures—one of Jesus and two "spirit portraits" of Pasteur and Lister* Somewhat incongruously, there is a little woolly dog, white and blue, on the mantelpiece. By the side of the door there is an empty plate with the inscription, "Free offerings for Sanctuary Funds."

We sit there waiting. From time to time the door opens to admit other patients, some of them very old and very sick indeed. They are all swallowed up in the tense silence. Somewhere in the distance there is the rapturous song of a canary.

The door opens and in strides Edwards, followed by three white-coated assistants, one man and two women. I felt what the others evidently felt—an instantaneous elevation of the spirit. The man was luminous with health. Not that there was anything aggressive or "hearty" about him; it was like a quality of light; his entry into the room had been like the drawing up of a blind.

He sat down in front of a Chinese screen. In spite of his white hair he looked about forty. (He is in fact fifty-seven). He had blue eyes of piercing clarity, a very clear skin, a winning smile. Without further more ado he motioned me to his side.

"Please ask any questions that occur to you," he said. "Now, who's first."

The first case was not sensational. It was an elderly man suffering from thrombosis. He had seen Edwards three weeks before, and had returned for a check-up before sailing home to South Africa.

"Have you been any better?" asked Edwards.

"Much better," said the man. The terrible pain had gone from his heart, and his blood pressure was nearly normal. (It must be remembered that all Edwards had done, on his previous visit, was to touch him with his hands.)

"I suppose you know that when you came to see me before, you

*These have since been removed.

had a clot?" said Edwards, placing the palm of his hand over the man's heart.

The man nodded. The doctors had told him so.

"Well, it's gone." He made a sweeping gesture across his chest. "And it won't return." He held out his hand. "Good-bye. Don't overdo things. And have a good trip."

It was as simple as that. Although this case was "not sensational" it is mentioned because my object is to present clear report of fact rather than an ecstatic elaboration of sensation. Sensational or not, from a strictly medical point of view, it was none the less singular. The patient was evidently a man of intelligence; and here he was, at an advanced age, testifying that the mere passing of Edwards's hand had lowered his blood pressure and removed an acute pain of long standing. Edwards now informed him that a clot had also been dissipated. There was, of course, no medical evidence for that claim, but in the light of what I was about to witness I should not be inclined to doubt it.

"Next, please."

In the nearest seat to us was a middle-aged Negro, black as black, shabbily dressed. I had noticed him as soon as I came in, because he was obviously in great pain and seemed to have difficulty in lifting his head.

The Negro shifted in his seat and rolled the whites of his eyes, which was the best he could do to attract attention.

"Next, please."

Edwards beckoned to him; he shuffled forward. As he took his place in the chair he seemed to sit more erect.

"What's the trouble?"

The Negro passed his hand eloquently over his abdomen. "It's my bowels, sir," he whispered. "For ten years I have such pain that I often cannot hold up my head."

Edwards stretched out his hand. The Negro flinched and drew back.

"I shan't hurt you."

Gently Edwards rested his hand on the man's stomach. As he did so I watched his face. It had a strange expression, as though he were *listening* for something. Although his fingers were moving, they seemed hardly to belong to him. In all the treatments I was to observe, there was always this sense of listening; it was as though he had a telephone receiver at his ear, and as though a voice were speaking from a great distance.

After some thirty seconds—not more—he lifted his hand from the abdomen to the back. There were a few swift gestures and then he had finished.

"Well," he said briskly, "that didn't take long."

The Negro stared at him with his huge mouth gaping; very tentatively he pushed a finger into his stomach, and began to grin; pushed harder; the grin spread all over his face.

"Go on," said Edwards. "*Try* to hurt yourself. Can you?"

The Negro slapped his stomach. "No, sir."

"Let's see if *I* can." Swiftly Edwards gave him a sharp punch. The Negro gave a delighted giggle.

"Did that hurt?"

"No, sir. Not at all, sir."

"Next, please."

It had all happened so swiftly that it had the quality of an illusion. *Was* it, in fact, just that? If healing could come like this, with the mere passing of a hand, could there have been anything really radical to heal? Had there, in other words, been anything really the matter with the man? You had only to look at him to answer that. His face was marked with the deep lines of the accumulated pain of a decade. And men, whether they are black or white, do not spend years grimacing with pain just for the fun of it.

"Next, please."

A little girl in a red dress was led forward by her mother. She was a pretty child, about five years old, but she walked oddly, as though her feet did not quite belong to her. As she climbed on to the chair her mother explained, rather tearfully, that in spite of four years' hospital treatment the doctors had told her that the child's legs would have to be put into irons.

"She was born with this, of course," said Edwards, looking at the child and not touching her.

The mother nodded.

Edwards turned to me. "I'd like you to feel this child's foot." I hesitated. "Go on. You will not hurt her."

I stretched out my hand and held the foot, closing my fingers round it. It was cool and white and tiny but it felt as though, inside it, there was a block of wood.

"Now let's see what we can do."

Edwards took the foot and gently stroked it. There was no question of anything so drastic as "manipulation", even "massage" would be far too strong a term; it was more the sort of thing one would do to comfort a child who had bruised herself.

I timed this "treatment" by my wrist-watch; it lasted just under ten seconds.

"Feel that," said Edwards, handing me the foot.

I closed my fingers round it once more. It was difficult to believe it was the same foot. All the stiffness had gone; it was as supple as a willow twig.

Before I had time to make any comments, Edwards, who had been gently stroking the other foot, observed to the mother, with a smile: "I don't think you need think any more about those irons." And then, to the little girl: "Now jump down and stand on your toes."

She jumped down, paused a moment, and then lifted herself on her toes. Not with any effort, and certainly with no sign of pain, but naturally and gaily with legs straight as an arrow and the arches erect.

By now, I was—to put it mildly—impressed. So were all the other people in the room. Some of the women had tears in their eyes; on the faces of others there was a look of ecstasy. But Edwards, throughout, remained quite calm and matter-of-fact. There was never a hint of theatrical gesture, nor a syllable of mystical patter. When I said to him—referring to the little girl who was standing on her toes—that was "a miracle", he merely shrugged his shoulders.

Nor did he claim to do the impossible . . . though he *was* doing the medically impossible. He gives no promises in advance that a patient will be cured. Indeed, in the next case, he stressed the fact that he could do little. This was the case of a very old lady who had hobbled in on two sticks. She must have been nearing ninety; she was bent almost double with rheumatoid arthritis; and she took so long getting across the room, even on the arms of the two assistants, that Edwards had plenty of time to explain his point of view before she was close enough to hear him.

"With this old lady," he said in a low voice, "there is practically nothing for me to work with. The shell of her body has worn so thin and grown so brittle that a breath of wind would crack it. All I can do is to give her a bit of warmth and comfort."

But he did much more than that, even with this tiny, tormented husk of a woman. She was a lovable little creature, with a quick and lively brain; although she was physically so grotesque she was still very feminine, with a strange, tragic echo of coquetry. Her hands were like knotted roots, her arms were set and stiff. "It is a bore," she said, with an agonised smile, "because I cannot move my arms to do my hair."

Her hair! Those few grey wisps over a yellowing skull!

"Let's see," said Edwards.

With extraordinary delicacy he touched her shoulders. She flinched.

"I'm not hurting you."

She flinched again.

"You *know* I'm not hurting you."

A flicker of a smile. "I suppose you're not."

"Then why do you make those faces?"

She shrugged her shoulders. Even as she did so, a look of astonishment came over her face.

"They moved! My shoulders!"

"Well . . . why not?"

"I . . . I don't know."

He drew her close to him. It was a strange sight, the white-coated, virile, vibrant man and the tiny, agonised bundle of diseased womanhood. He passed his hands down her spine. This was not done in silence . . . there were comforting words from him, and protesting, even petulant words from her. I cannot remember them and I do not propose to invent them. All that I remember is that at the end—and the whole process lasted less than three minutes—he leant back and said:

"Well, you can do your hair *now*."

The nearly skeleton arms were raised, of their own accord, to the grey wisps. The knotted fingers patted them. She nodded and smiled. It was a very ancient smile, a flicker on the edge of the tomb, but it was not a smile of pain.

I must stress one essential point.

In all these proceedings there was no hint of "manipulation". I have said that before, but it must be said again. If Edwards had been achieving these results by a sort of super-osteopathy it would have been remarkable but it would not have been magical, and that is a word from which it is impossible to escape. Consider the next case—an advanced condition of curvature of the spine.

"I'd like you to put your hands on this woman's back," said Edwards.

I got up, and placed the palm of my hand where the assistant directed.

"Feel it?"

I nodded. In the centre of the back the spine bulged out to the left in a sort of arc; one needed no knowledge of anatomy to realise that it was grossly mis-shapen.

"Now wait a minute."

He drew the woman to him; it was a kind of mingling of two bodies; his hands moved gently over her back, not pressing, not twisting—merely gliding. In less than a minute he released her.

"Feel that spine now," he said.

It was as straight as a ruler. One would have said that only a surgical operation or the prolonged use of brute force could have achieved such a transformation. But the woman, apparently, had not felt a flicker of discomfort. She had been healed—but pain had played no part in the healing.

Accounts of miracles can become monotonous, so I will give only one more example.

Sitting before us was a woman who, quite obviously, was in deep distress. She was what I would call a dim woman, in every sense of the word; dim in features, in clothes, in voice, in personality; dim in everything but pain; one had a feeling that all the colour had been washed out of her by years of suffering.

"How can I help you?"

The woman whispered that she had three troubles; a perpetual pain in her back; a gastric ulcer; and an acute sinus which had been completely blocked for eight years.

Edwards dealt quickly with the first two troubles, leaving the sinus till the last.

"How many times have they operated on this?" he asked quietly.

"Three."

He stretched out his hand and stroked her face. It was then that there came that touch of drama which, quite frankly, I need, in order to bring these things home to you; and the drama consisted merely in a sound, the gentle sound of air being drawn in through the nostrils. When Edwards touched that woman's face her nose had been blocked for eight years. In spite of three operations, in spite of all the pain and laceration of the flesh, she had been unable to breathe normally. He touched her, and said: "Now breathe."

She closed her dim pallid mouth and took a deep breath. I leant forward. I could hear the long, steady intake of air through the normal channels. It seemed one of the strangest sounds I have ever heard. The woman's face flushed; a little sparkle came into her eyes.

"Anything wrong with that?"

The woman shook her head; she was too moved to speak.

"Your nervous condition is bad. You need a little help." He motioned to the white-frocked assistant, Olive Burton, by his side. She stood by her, closing her eyes, touching her. As with Edwards, one felt she was listening.

When the woman got up to go, she was breathing normally. She had no pain, and she was no longer "dim". She had come back to life.

At the end of the healing session, which lasted nearly three hours, I went to Edwards's study to have a cup of tea.

"You weren't disappointed?"

"Hardly."

"You must remember that the great majority of the people we try to heal have been given up as incurable. If you're writing anything about us, you might stress that point."

"I will."

"You might also mention that most of our work is done by absent healing. It would be physically impossible for me to be personally present at every case of healing. We received our millionth letter this week. Yes—our millionth, in four years. I reply to every letter, and I use such powers as are given to me to help those who write. They are helped by my spirit, not by my body. Or rather, by the spirits who use me."

"But is absent healing as effective as what I have seen today?" For answer he pushed a portfolio across the desk.

"In that folder," he said, "are over five hundred cases of 'incurable' cancer which have been healed by our intervention in the last four years. Each of those cases is attested by qualified medical evidence. You might care to glance through it."

I took the folder and began to study it. (Edwards afterwards allowed me to take it home, and it is before me as I write.) It is an anthology of miracles. The word is not mine; it is used with monotonous frequency by the doctors and nurses in the cases concerned. "This miraculous recovery" . . . "The patient is the amazement of the doctors" . . . "This case is making history in the hospital" . . . etc. etc.

I am inclined to take a firm grip of my pen when writing of so cruel an enemy as cancer, lest I should write anything to arouse false hopes. That would be a crime; but surely it would also be a crime, even if there were only a fraction of truth in this dosier—and the evidence in it seems to me incontestable—to refrain from doing all one could to publicise it. One curious feature of these cancer cases interested me, as a layman, and that was the physical technique by which some of the growths were dissolved. In many cases, at the crucial period, an exceptional mass of alien matter was evacuated through the rectum; at other times, notably in cancer of the breast, there was violent perspiration. Is it unduly fanciful to suggest that this physical technique is in harmony with the psychic theory by which Edwards explains this phenomena? By what other theory than the casting-out of devils are we to account for it? However, Edwards views such casting-out to refer more to cases of mental disorder and obsessions.

It is when we come to examine this "psychic theory by which Edwards explains the phenomena" that most people will find themselves up against hurdles which their minds—or maybe their spirits—are unable to surmount. Briefly, it is that Edwards is controlled by various doctors in the spirit world, notably Lister and Pasteur, who use him as a channel through which they pour the unlimited healing resources of the Infinite. That is the simplest way of stating the essentials of the process. There are many minor, or perhaps it would be better to say supplementary miracles involved in it, such as the art of "spirit travelling", by which he can

Platform—at Royal Festival Hall

Supported by the white-coated members of the National Federation of Spiritual Healers, Harry Edwards addresses the gathering

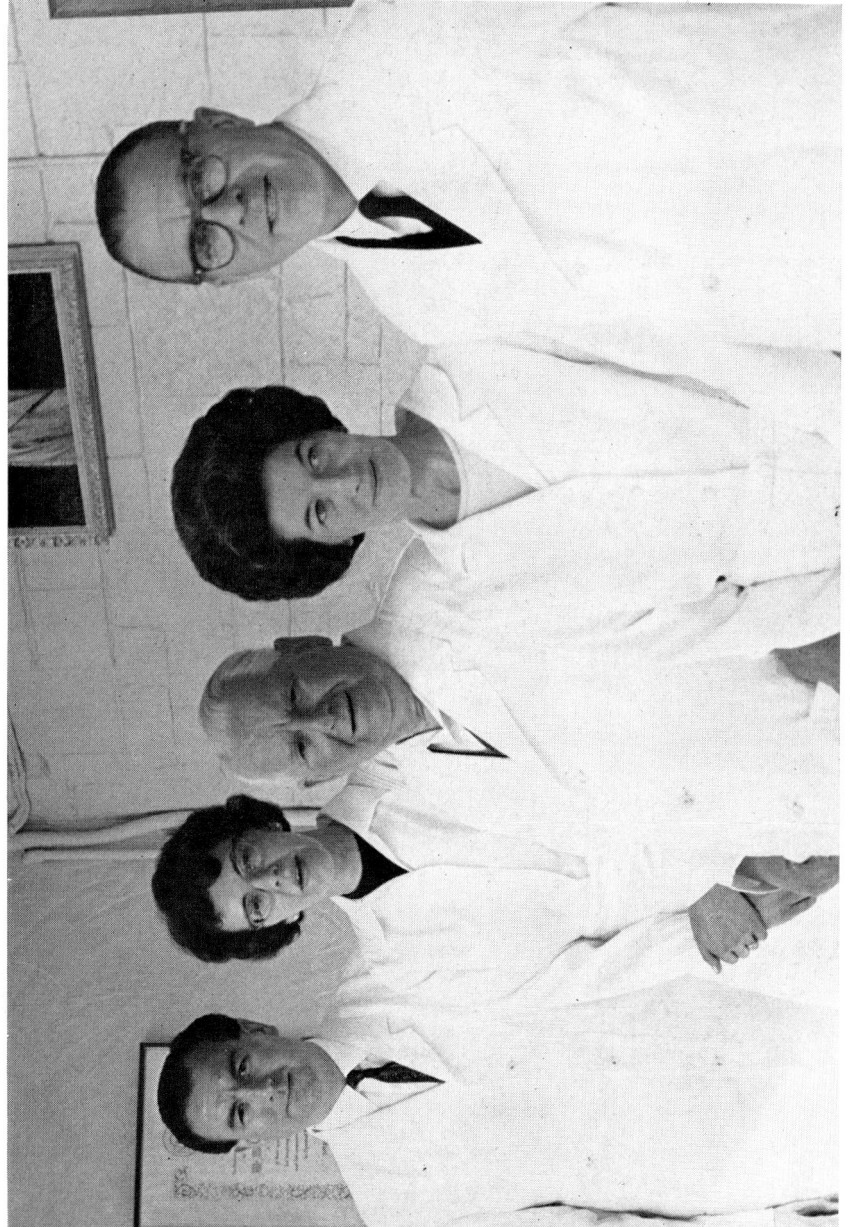

The Healing Team

project his spirit to distant hospitals and sick rooms. This whole, strange, bewildering affair has been organised, after many years of experience, on a strictly businesslike basis. By which, I do *not* mean that the Sanctuary is a money-making concern. A healer must live, and if those he has healed like to give him something to help him carry on, Edwards is grateful. But he accepts indifferently the rich and poor, and he never asks for money.

What I mean by "businesslike" is that the whole technique of his healing is organised on a rational basis, that the vast correspondence—3,500 letters a week—are carefully read and annotated, that the secretaries are efficiently trained and that—if I may say so without an appearance of flippancy—that the services of the late Lord Lister and the late Monsieur Pasteur are taken as much for granted, at the Sanctuary, as if they were resident members of a hospital staff.

Well—there we are. To sum up, I would suggest that whichever way you look at it, you are confronted by a miracle. If you reject the psychic interpretation, you have to explain away the healing of multitudes of "incurables". If you are supremely sceptical, and reject the healing itself, you have to explain away the phenomena of multitudes of people who *think* they have been healed, and who behave as if they were healed, and go on believing as if they were healed for the rest of their natural lives. Which really is carrying scepticism to extremes.

We will end this piece by returning for a moment to the Sanctuary; I want to mention one last little piece of evidence which, though homely, is significant.

I said good-bye to Edwards, got into the car and headed for home. It was a lovely evening; the lanes were sunlit, the birds in full song. It was half past six; I felt happy; it would be pleasant to stop at an inn and drink a glass of beer and scribble a few notes while all these things were fresh in my memory. I mention the glass of beer for two reasons; first as evidence that I was not floating in a sort of etherial mist, but was still very much a creature of this world; secondly, because as I drank it, the barman made a remark which may serve as a tailpiece to this story.

I had my drink in a cool, empty room in the Trust House at Shere.

"Been up to Burrows Lea?" said the barman.

"Yes."

"Makes you think, doesn't it?"

"It does indeed."

The barman nodded, and drew on his pipe. "All the same," he said, "if you want real proof, you don't want to go to Burrows Lea. You want to go down to the station at Dorking."

"To the station? Why?"

The barman grinned. "To talk to the porters. Dorking's the station where they all come. All the cripples, all the hopeless ones. The porters see 'em come. And the porters see 'em go. You wouldn't believe they were the same. You ask the porters."

"They see 'em come and they see 'em go." Yes, I thought. The Dorking porters must have an interesting job. But I had no need to call their evidence; I had seen it myself.

CHAPTER ELEVEN

HEALING IN STRANGE PLACES

SPIRITUAL healing sanctuaries are hallowed places. Healers, whenever they can, arrange for a place to be set apart for this purpose and for no other. It may be a small room in the private dwelling-house dedicated to healing, and most likely will have a table with a cross upon it and some fresh flowers. There will be found no disturbing picture, object or motif but whatever adornments there may be would be suggestive of a spiritual nature. A sanctuary becomes a revered place both to the healer and his patients, possessing an atmosphere of sacredness.

In a church, there may be a healing room or the healing may take place in the church itself, before the altar.

It is thought by many that the Sanctuary at Burrows Lea, Shere, is ideal. It is set far from the road amidst the most peaceful surroundings. It is quiet; no other sounds but the singing of the birds can be heard. It is never used for anything other than healing and meditation. When people enter into it, they sense its hallowedness and are reverent and quiet.

Healing under these conditions is ideal, but at times it has to take place under quite the reverse conditions.

I recall holding a healing service in a London town hall. The main assembly hall adjoined the magistrates' court—a cold, sinister sort of place, with the dock, jury boxes, etc. When the public healing service was over, we had to adjourn into the courtroom to give treatment to cases that were unseen during the main service. A more unspiritual place it would be hard to imagine, but nevertheless healing was given.

It was here that I had an experience that shocked me deeply. I was giving healing treatment to a man almost totally incapacitated from disseminated sclerosis. From the waist down he was paralysed; his legs were heavy and inert, and he had not been able to stand or walk for a long time. He was accompanied by his wife. As the healing proceeded we were able to restore mobility to his "poker-back" spine, to impart new strength to his legs, and observe the first signs of returning co-ordination. He was able to stand up from his wheel-chair by himself and to do so without falling. Then under gentle direction he was encouraged to make a few walking steps, supported, to overcome his poor sense of balance. But he *was* walking again. Medically the man was totally incurable, but in a short time we were able to observe the paralysis yielding to the healing. The man was overjoyed and for a few moments, his reserve broke down with joy at being able to walk once again.

With such cases as this, we expect to see gradual improvement come as the days pass by, providing the patient can receive loving care and help from his dear ones. Home massage is recommended to stimulate the circulation and help restore vitality to the muscles that have been idle for so long. Morale needs to be encouraged to keep the patient's outlook positive and persevering.

We always show the relative or friend who accompanies the patient how to give massage, and how the patient can be further helped at home each day to seek improved co-ordination by "talking", as it were, to the limbs—to encourage the brain to pass messages down through the nerves and so induce a muscular response.

So it was, on this occasion in the foreboding atmosphere of the police court, I turned to the wife, to ask her to do this. I showed her how her husband could now stand up and sit down by himself and make a few walking steps, and I asked her if she would help him each day to maintain the improvements and seek for further improvement, assuring her that the healing would continue through absent healing. It was her attitude to her husband and the dead sort of voice that shocked me, when she said with a shrug of her shoulders, "I've had him like this for years and I'm fed up with him."

It may be understandable under the circumstances. The wife had to go to work to earn money to keep the home going. To greet her when she returned home at the end of the day, there was an inert hulk of a body that needed everything to be done for it, and with difficulty too; in addition to all her other household and cooking duties. While I could appreciate the situation, it was the entire lack of feeling the wife showed that disturbed me. Even when she saw, for the first time in years, her husband stand up on his feet and make the few new steps in walking again, there was no response in her—just that dead look and indifference of voice that was so hurtful.

One day, when I was healing at Ewell in Surrey, a taxi drew up at the door. A woman got out and asked me if I could help her brother, who was mentally afflicted. I asked her to bring him in, but she said he would not come, so would I go out to see him. I went with her to the taxicab and we got in, where I sat facing him.

The story of this healing is similar to the healing of the doctor's son, described in Chapter Four. When I sat down, there was no acknowledgement of my presence at all and his eyes looked "far away". I guessed him to be about twenty-five years of age. He wanted the taxicab to get going, so the cabby was told to drive around. I began to talk to the man, but got no answer. Then I noticed his right arm was limp and hanging forward—it was partially paralysed, probably an ill-effect following a convulsion or a fit. I took his hand in mine and asked him to grip my hand. At first there was no response, but as I encouraged him to try again, so I felt the signs of the grip returning. Next, I encouraged his arm to move, backwards, forwards and then upwards, and I felt the act of fulfilling my requests. Suddenly he said: "That's good!"

When he said these words, his sister became excited and exclaimed: "They are the first clear words you have said for ages." His reply was simple and natural, as he said, "I know."

As I persevered with his arm and encouraged him to talk, it became apparent that a noticeable change was taking place. His eyes began to look intelligent, his voice gathered strength and assurance, and a smile came to his face.

He asked me: "Can I do my buttons up and can I strike a match?" As the taxi moved through the streets, he tried to button up his coat and found he could do so without very much trouble, just a little fumbling. I borrowed a box of matches from the taxi-man. Lighting a match was difficult at first for the box slipped from his fingers. With encouragement he was able to hold the box firmly for the length of time necessary for his good hand to take out a match and strike it. I gave him a cigarette and he lit this from a match without any help.

Most remarkable was the change in his facial expression, it became "alive" and his eyes became observant. A few weeks later his sister told me how tremendously better he was and that he had been accepted back in his old firm.

As that taxicab drove through the streets no one knew of the "drama" taking place within it. We were taken back to my place and as I got out the driver said to me, "I've seen some strange things take place in my cab, but now I've seen everything."

Every two or three months we used to conduct healing services on Sunday evenings at the Victoria Halls in Bloomsbury under the aegis of the Spiritualist Society of Great Britain. In those days it was customary for us to stay behind after the service to give healing to all the rest of the people who needed it. We adopted this practice to allay feelings of disappointment with those who had come hoping for treatment and which time did not permit during the service itself. Later, we were compelled to discontinue this, for the conditions became unsuitable for healing; we were besieged by a large number of people without any discipline or order.

So one night, we told the sick to line up on the pavement. The people formed up in a long queue, and so healing was given this way (perhaps for the first time ever) in a London street. Even this had to be stopped because we were said to be creating a breach of the peace.

On Whit-Sunday, 1964, we conducted the first open-air spiritual healing demonstration on the plinth of Nelson's Column in Trafalgar Square, London, before an estimated audience of three thousand people. This was successful with obvious changes for the better being clearly observed with a number of afflicted people. One young man suffering from paralysis following polio-meningitis, was able to discard his caliper and walk. A spastic child was able to move his arms upright, which had been impossible before. Another man whose shoulder was semi-locked from arthritis was able to move it freely and swing it round and round as well as to push the arm upwards in an erect position.

A film, entitled *The Healing Spirit* (which has been shown all over the world), was made from this Trafalgar Square demonstration, in which it followed up the progress the healing had initiated.

The young man with the caliper was shown taking his dog out for a walk, minus the caliper. The child was shown holding and waving a rattle. The man with the locked shoulder was filmed cleaning a window using his arm freely and naturally. Other cases were followed up showing that freedom from affliction had been maintained. These Trafalgar Square healing services have become an annual event and have been continued every Whit-Sunday since.

I have given healing to patients in public houses, in the street, in meetings, corridors, and indeed everywhere, including lavatories.

The last experience I will mention took place during the last war on a gunsite on Clapham Common. I was then in the Home Guard, and one of our duties was to undertake guard duties around the anti-aircraft battery of four powerful guns. At this time I was a private, later on becoming a Lieutenant Platoon Commander.

One night, we were on duty when the blitz on London was at its height. The guns were firing at the enemy aeroplanes overhead; they were in continuous action, shaking the ground we were standing on. Searchlights pierced the sky which was pock-marked by the exploding shells, and lit up into an angry red glare from buildings on fire.

The sergeant in charge of the guard and I were standing in the open looking at this amazing spectacle, when he told me he had an eye disease of long standing which necessitated his going to the eye hospital every week for treatment. He knew about my gift of healing, and so it was that on this gunsite, with the guns blazing away, I placed my hands over the sergeant's eyes and sought for healing to reach them. When the sergeant next went to the hospital on his weekly visit, it was seen that the eyes had almost cleared and soon after they were completely free from trouble.

Quite apart from healing, there is another story of interest to a student of human nature and it may well answer the question arising in the mind of a reader concerning the above story of the healing of the sergeant's eye disease, namely, how is it possible to disassociate one's mind from scenes of intense activity, such as during the firing of heavy guns only a few yards away?

Our Home Guard had a small wooden hut to house and sleep the sentries when not on duty. Every time one of the guns were fired the hut seemed to jump up in the air. When all the guns were in continuous action those inside the hut were literally shaken up and down. Our rifles and all impedimenta, cups, etc., had to be secured or they would fly about the hut like poltergeist activity. We became so accustomed to this that the men would sleep through the inferno of noise and vibrations.

One evening, therefore, when we arrived at the gunsite, a continuous blitz was on and the guns were being fired constantly. For a while the members of the guard stood around watching the amazing spectacle. The flash and roar of the guns; the droning of the enemy aeroplanes overhead; the explosions in the air as the shells burst; the weaving searchlights; the red glow of fires; the falling of the bombs and the crash they made breaking down buildings. It seemed as if we were in the very centre of it all. I remember wondering at the time what a lot of money some people might pay for such an experience.

After standing around watching all this going on with the crash of the four heavy guns going off only a stone's throw away, the men would get tired of watching the spectacle and go in the hut to read magazines or to talk. When I looked in, I heard one Home Guardsman quite seriously say to another: "If you snore tonight, Abrahams, I'll pour a bucket of water over you." Apparently, the noise of the guns going off did not matter, the hut being bumped up and down was of little consequence, but for Abrahams to snore, was positively unendurable!

CHAPTER TWELVE

THE LESSON OF THE V 1 BOMB

IN the years preceding the last war and during the first war years, an ever-increasing number of sick people wrote to me for absent healing or came to my house for personal treatment. I had converted one room into a healing sanctuary and we were giving treatment seven evenings a week.

The number of sufferers who came in person became so great that our front room and sanctuary could not accommodate them all and queues formed outside in the street. As I had to work in the day time at my printing and stationery business the healing could only take place in the evenings, and in addition to this the requests for absent healing multiplied. I was therefore compelled to institute a system of appointments for personal healing and leave some evenings free for absent healing.

The successful and high percentage of recoveries taking place through absent healing showed me this should become my major concern. At that time, I followed the absent healing methods adopted by other healers and made a time appointment with my correspondents to link up with the absent healing intercession at a set time. I believed in this process, and valued my timetable register very highly. I thought it essential that the patient should sit quietly during the precise minutes we were interceding for him.

In those days tuberculosis was still "the great white scourge", and I noted continuous outstanding success with the healing of this disease, so much so that I was able to foretell the way in which the healing would progress. As a rule, the patients were in sanatoria, with high temperatures and pronounced infection. Thus, when I received a request for absent healing for a tubercular patient I began to look for changes taking place to a regular pattern. By the first or second week, the temperature would come down to normal; then, as tests were made, it would be discovered that all active signs of infection had disappeared. Then would follow improvement with the respiration and cessation of phlegm and congestion. Finally, the general health tone would build up once again and it would not be long before the patient was discharged or sent to a convalescent home.

Some interesting situations developed and I often had tussles with some of the doctors. I recall one case of a man whose lung showed on the X-ray photographic plate a marked area of infection and scar tissue. Absent healing intervened and the next time the man's chest was photographed it showed the lung as being quite free from trouble. The doctors could not understand this but were determined to find out where the diseased area had gone. They carried out every test they could, even to photographing internally the whole area of the lung square inch by square inch. Of course, they could not find it, and declared that the tubercular condition had "gone into hiding".

I was informed on a number of occasions, that following a successful healing of tuberculosis with the disappearance of all symptoms and infection, the doctors would insist on carrying out the full-scale two- or three-year treatment and even surgery. I remember one special case in which a contest developed between the doctor, the patient and myself.

The patient was a lady who had tuberculosis in both lungs. She was too weak for surgery and the respirations were so little that one lung could not be collapsed. Absent healing was asked for, and, following the usual course, the temperature came down and tests showed that the infection was no longer active. Her vitality and strength improved with fuller respirations, all the other symptoms disappeared.

When I commenced absent healing for her, I outlined the progressive nature of the healing, telling her what signs of betterment to look out for. She was able to observe this orderly progress within her condition, and her doctors confessed their bewilderment and their inability to understand how the lady had recovered from a very chronic condition. Nevertheless, they told her they intended to carry on with the full-scale treatment, including the thoracoplasty operation, as a precautionary measure.

THE LESSON OF THE V1 BOMB

The lady became very indignant, and she wrote me an urgent letter asking me to get into touch with the doctor to explain the means by which she had recovered and to question the necessity for surgery.

I wrote to the medical superintendent of the hospital, giving him a detailed explanation of the healing pattern, and quoted other cases in support of my claims.

I received a rather angry letter in reply, describing my letter as an impertinence and pointing out that I had no right to question a medical opinion or to influence a patient against a doctor's judgement.

In reply, I gave the doctor a number of case histories, with names, addresses, hospitals and even the doctors' names attending those patients, simply requesting the medical superintendent to contact the other hospitals and the doctors for verification, to ascertain whether there was not a case for consideration and research.

I heard no more from the doctor, who had then given an ultimatum to the lady patient either to submit to surgery or to be discharged from hospital, in which case the doctor would accept no further responsibility for her. She chose to be discharged.

In order to give some protection to the lady, I arranged a compromise with the medical superintendent (using the bait that he would naturally wish to see how his patient fared) for him to see the lady at intervals to check-up her condition. She went every three months for this check-up and each time was given a clean bill. This continued for a year, when she was told that she need not attend any more.

I wrote a final letter to the doctor, quoting his previous letters, and again suggested it would be in the common interest to review the cases of patients who had been cured to see whether cooperation with spiritual healing could be used for other sufferers. I had no response. I kept in touch with the lady concerned for a considerable time afterwards, and she never had any relapse. Every Christmas for years after she would send me a Christmas card to show me she was well.

Here is another case of medical unreasonableness. A man who had been doing some part-time work for me at home, typing letters, found that his neck suddenly became fixed and was exceedingly painful. He went to a hospital in Guildford and was at once admitted as an in-patient.

He was there for a number of weeks, receiving different forms of treatment including physiotherapy, traction and manipulation under an anaesthetic, but all to no purpose. Then one morning the doctor in charge of his case sent him home with the comment "to give you a rest from treatment". Clearly, he could do no more for him.

On leaving the hospital he came straight away to see me. It only took a few moments to free the neck so that it could bend, turn and move freely in all directions without a sign of discomfort. The man was so delighted, he went straight back to the hospital, sought out his doctor, and showed him that his neck was free from trouble by moving it up and down and from side to side.

"What have you done to it?" asked the doctor.

"I've been to see Mr. Harry Edwards at Shere and he has put it right."

To this the doctor replied: "Mr. Coates, you are a man of common sense, surely you don't believe in all that nonsense?"

This made Mr. Coates rather angry, and he indignantly retorted:

"You've had me in hospital for six weeks and could not help me. Only a few hours ago you sent me home, in pain, to have a rest from treatment. I saw Mr. Edwards and he has done what you could not, for my neck is now quite free and all the pain has gone."

The doctor angrily shut down his desk with a bang and shouted: "Get out of here!"

Returning to the good progress the healing work was making during the last war years, one day, just before lunch-time, a V1 bomb descended and exploded very near to my house, blowing off part of the roof and knocking down the front walls and other parts of the house. Almost all of our home was a mass of rubble and my record book and healing register were destroyed.

In losing that healing register it was as if the very bottom had fallen out of life itself, for I knew that the absent healing work had received a very heavy blow. All I could then do was to recall from my memory as many cases as I could for directive intercession and conduct a mass intercession for the remainder.

I anticipated a marked falling off in the good progress patients were reporting but to my astonishment I found that instead of the percentage of improvements decreasing, it was actually increasing. This was contrary to what I had anticipated and caused me to review all that I had been doing in healing practice. After this, I questioned everything I did in the light of common sense and what I then knew about the science of spiritual healing. There is no need for me to go into further detail in this book, for I have done so in others. Suffice it to say, therefore, that from that time onwards until the present day I have never made any timed absent healing appointments, except under special circumstances.

The destruction of my home also taught me another important lesson. There was a man afflicted with paralysis who came every Friday afternoon for personal treatment and I would leave my business premises and go home specially to see him. He had been making excellent progress and was able to see for himself the perceptible restoration of co-ordination and function within the paralysed limbs.

On the Friday afternoon following the destruction of my house, this man came into my shop, looking very dejected. I could see the despair in his eyes for he thought he would not be able to have any further treatment; but we withdrew into the printing works, where I continued his treatment, to his great happiness.

When this man, so downcast, came into the shop, I felt within me a powerful impression that relatively it was of far more importance for that man to have his healing than the fact that my home was now a pile of rubble.

It was a lesson in *real values* that from then on became one of my guiding principles in life.

CHAPTER THIRTEEN

DISTANCE NO OBJECT

We have found that many physical afflictions arise from a spinal defect, the most common of which is the notorious "slipped disc"; but general lesions, stiffness in any form and, of course, even a mild curvature, can bring about lumbago, sciatica, paralysis, fibrositis, and even loss of control over bowel and bladder action. Sometimes a spine has become so rigid as to earn the description of "poker-back".

Some of these troubles become so deep-seated that various medical treatments can do little to overcome them and they then enter the "incurable" category. Generally, however, such conditions yield easily to spiritual healing, and this particularly applies to slipped discs, the latter only very rarely failing to be cured by this means.

Time after time, we have seen patients doubled over with pain, slowly and agonisingly, dragging their steps as they enter the Sanctuary on the arms of their friends.

Within a minute or two, they are flexing their backs freely in all directions, standing up straight, bending over to touch their toes, lifting weights and so on, quite free from pain or stress. I have lost count of the patients so healed over the years, for their numbers must run into many thousands, the same story being related in the field of healership everywhere. To recall a number of stories of spinal healings would only be repetitive and boring, so I will be content with telling just two.

The first concerns a Mr. John Sellars of New Zealand who had a small factory business. For five years he had suffered spinal torture from his neck down through his spine, crippling his limb movements. He had been an in-patient in hospitals several times and his spine had been operated upon. He had further been encased in plaster; suffered traction, and had been finally discharged as "incurable" having been fitted with a steel reinforced leather corset and another contraption to support and hold his head in a fixed position. He could only get about slowly and painfully with the aid of elbow crutches.

Mr. Sellars had read of the healing work at Burrows Lea and became conscious of an intense desire to come to England to receive healing from us. He had no money to permit this, but so great was his conviction that we could help him that he sold up his business, his house, and his home to get the necessary money needed for the journey for him and his wife.

The day arrived when they came to the Sanctuary, and when it was his turn for treatment he made a very sorry sight as he came painfully towards us. He was wearing the heavy leather and plastic collar around his neck and assisted by his wife, he could only shuffle along using his two elbow crutches.

He was eased down on to the stool before me, his wife taking his crutches, and with support from Mr. Burton was able to sit, although bent right over. As I placed my arms around him I could feel the unyielding steel-braced corset, tightly laced, stretching from his shoulders right down to his thighs.

He told me the tragic story of his medical history, and I could sense his coming to us in great faith. I told him that I could give him no promise or undertaking that he would be healed, but that we would seek help for him and would cause him no pain.

First I removed the imprisoning collar, which went down over his shoulders and had an extending arm over and down his chest. It was no simple task to do this, but with help from his wife we succeeded.

With one hand on his neck and the other on his forehead, I first encouraged him to just nod his head and from this to extend the movement, bone by bone, down his neck. Soon the first four bones were palpating nicely under my fingers. The remaining three neck bones were arching outwards, but as I asked him to let his head go gently right back, telling him to look at the ceiling, so I felt the protruding bones align with the others and move with freedom. The head could then pivot round from side to side loosely, he could bring his chin down to his chest and arch the head backwards to the full extent, freely and with no pain at all.

Next, I turned to his spine and found there was sufficient room within the corset to obtain the movements I sought for. It is interesting to note that we invariably carry out the freeing of locked spines with the patients wearing their steel braces and plaster or leather corsets. When doctors have watched us do this it is incomprehensible to them that we should even try to treat a spine without the patient being stripped. This also provides evidence that spinal healings through spiritual healing are not "manipulations".

Mr. Sellars's spine yielded easily, and with the movement possible within the corset he could bend his back, forwards, arching backwards, sideways, and rotating, without feeling even one twinge of pain.

I loosed all his leg joints. He was then able to stand up from a sitting position normally. He could lift his knees up and stand on tip-toes. He could walk perfectly without the need of his crutches or any support.

His healing was successful and complete. I advised him to return to his hotel, obtain an ordinary belt support for his back, to avoid him getting a chill in it and to give a little support after wearing the steel corset for so long. He did this, and told me he was well in every way—he had had no more pain.

Having used up all his money, he and his wife went to friends in Scotland where they both found employment to save up money for their return fares to New Zealand. Before they returned they paid a second visit to the Sanctuary for a check-up and to express their gratitude.

About a year later, I received a letter from Mr. Sellars in which he wrote:

"I don't know if you will remember me or not, but I am the man who came all the way from New Zealand for healing to your Sanctuary and despite the fact that it was your day off, you still gave me healing and therefore put me back on the road to health and strength again. I was able to pay a second visit to the Sanctuary for you to see how complete was my cure.

"Well, I have now settled down in New Zealand again, and I may say my friends and colleagues at work are absolutely amazed at the difference in me—as when I went to the United Kingdom I was a very pitiful sight. I had a brace on my neck and one on

The Healing Sanctuary, Burrows Lea, Shere, Guildford, Surrey

After a few minutes healing an "incurable" is able to walk unaided. (Picture from *The Power of Spiritual Healing*)

my spine and had had five years of in and out of hospital for operations and plaster casts, etc. I had to walk with the aid of sticks.

"I am now 100 per cent, and feel as fit as a fiddle and now that I am settled I thought I would take this opportunity of writing to thank you and your helpers for everything you have done for me—but how can mere words express the gratitude I feel—they just cannot."

The second case of healing I will mention, occurred at the Royal Festival Hall, London. I had asked for sufferers from spinal curvature to put their hands up for me to select two people from. I saw a hand in the far distance and chose that one as one of the two.

The owner of the hand was an elderly man, who could not walk. He had to be carried by two stewards from his seat, down the body of the hall and on to the platform.

When he was seated before me, I got him to tell his story through the microphone to the audience. He said he was an engineer and some years ago had fallen into an engine pit, breaking his back. He was taken to hospital and was kept there for some time, where he had X-rays taken and had to lay fastened up for a number of weeks, incapable of movement. Finally he was discharged as incurable for nothing more could the doctors do for him.

As he told his story, I confess I felt concerned as to whether we should be able to effect any measurable cure. This happened to be the last patient that afternoon, and it does not leave a good impression to have a sufferer, whose condition is such that a recovery is not possible under the laws that govern us.

I had noted that he could not walk and soon found the reason why. His legs were completely paralysed and no movement could be induced. I then appreciated the spinal condition and found in the lumbar spine the bones projecting in a pronounced knob, where the backbone had been broken but was now fused together in a "lump". It seemed pretty hopeless and that I should have a failure.

I need not have worried. As I sought for mobility in the rest of the poker-back spine, I felt it yielding, I was conscious of it becoming mobile and then as I looked for the healing to reach the lumpy projection, I felt it yield and to disappear. His back was all right. This gave me confidence, and I asked him to raise one knee and then the other. He could do this, too. I lifted his feet in my hands and asked him to push down. This he did with strength. I knew then that the functioning of the nerves had been restored and the paralysis overcome.

I asked him to stand up—but he shook his head. I took his hands and helped him to stand. His look of amazement delighted the audience.

Then I said: "Lift up one knee." He did so. Then the other and so made his first new steps in walking. He did not need any further encouragement. He walked up and down the long platform. Then down the steps by himself and back to his seat at the rear of the hall, ascending the higher levels and gradient without faltering.

This healing was recorded by the Press photographers and the pictures were published in the Press. There were three pictures, one showing him being carried to the platform by two stewards; the second showing me healing his spine and the third of the man walking down the steps from the platform by himself, unaided.

In the 1950s a young couple bought a large farm in Kenya, which covered such an extensive territory that the only way of supervising the farm lands was on horse-back. This farm was a challenge to the courage, pertinacity and endurance of these young people. The wife played as constructive a part in the farm's management as her husband—until one day she became very ill, and was flown to London. The first part of her story is written in her own words:

"On August 16th, 1957, I was flown to London and the following day was taken by ambulance to Foredown Hospital, Portslade, Brighton, suffering from Bulba Polio. I was operated upon immediately for a tracheotomy. At the time I was unable to swallow liquid or food, my throat muscles being paralysed. Also I had lost the power of speech.

"In hospital I was being fed through a nose tube. My ability to breathe was extremely poor and the following day, August 18th, I was put on to an automatic breathing machine.

"At 9 a.m. on the morning of August 20th when my brother came to see me he was told that I was not expected to live more than another three hours. My aunt, Lady Baden Powell, on hearing this news contacted you at once at the Sanctuary, Shere, asking for your help.

"The paralysis by that time had affected my neck, my brain and the top half of my body was threatening to close in on my heart. My heart-beats were getting slower and slower. My left lung had stopped operating altogether and report has it that my eyes were completely sunken in a death-like mask.

"At 5 p.m. I was still alive. My mother arrived from Kenya and I was just able to recognise her. To the doctors and nurses attending me it was a miracle that I survived that day and the following night.

"I, personally, did not know until long after I was off the danger list—in fact until several months later—that you had been contacted and that you and your healers had been, and were giving me, spiritual help through absent healing.

"During the time that I was on the danger list—just under one month—it never once occurred to me that I should not pull through, nor indeed, that I was not expected to live.

"May I now quote from my mother's letters:

"August 21st. 'Angela seemed happier and brighter this evening when I was allowed to see her for longer. They say her spirits are good and that she is fighting hard.'

"(I was apparently continually asking for my aunt from whom I found I had always received mental strength.) 'Betty is having Angela prayed for and healed by Mr. Harry Edwards and his circle. Betty is confident that all will be well, and I think Angela must feel this strength in her.

"August 24th. 'These first two days she has really seemed brighter. Also she is more contented and has a tiny bit of colour in her cheeks.'

"August 26th. For the first time I was able to breathe without assistance, through the tube in my neck. 'The sisters say she has amazing will power and spirit.'

"September 9th. The first signs of life of my voice. Was able, with difficulty to speak my first few words. 'Angela is getting stronger and more cheerful in herself.'

"September 20th. Was able to lift my head two inches off the pillow. Beginning to speak more naturally.

"September 23rd. 'Angela is well out of the wood now and is

getting on like a house on fire. She sat up for one and a half hours yesterday and has been trying to walk. Yesterday, she managed to get nearly all round the room.'

"November 3rd. 'Angela has been making steady progress. She can eat the inside of toast now and has put on, at least, eight pounds.'

"November 26th. Left Foredown Hospital for a period of convalescence. Attending Reading Hospital for physiotherapy three times a week until the time we sailed for Kenya, in February this year.

"October, 1958. It would now be hard to tell that I've ever suffered from polio."

That is the end of the narrative, and some comments are worth while. It will be noted that absent healing was asked for, as a "last hope" emergency when Angela was hourly expected to die. I was kept informed about her every few days to enable the healing to be directive for her particular needs as the days went by. She did not die, but within three months she was discharged from hospital and now has no trace of polio or any of the distressing complications that invariably follow this disease.

I heard later on that Angela was riding over the wide area of the farm and carrying on exacting duties to assist her husband with the farm management.

This is an example of how spiritual healing combined with good medical treatment and nursing was able to heal a young woman who at the time the healing commenced was so near to leaving this life.

CHAPTER FOURTEEN

EVIDENTIAL HEALING

WHENEVER there is attunement with Spirit, healing can take place at all times. As an example, I will take the case of Edwina, the sixteen-year-old daughter of Mr. and Mrs. Burton, who, one evening, was with her mother in the kitchen while supper was being prepared on the electric cooker, the hot-plate of which is a circular metal-cased cable spiralling in to the centre. Mrs. Burton had a minute or two before switched off the cooker, the usual red-hot glow having gone, when Edwina, in a moment of distraction, leaned backwards against the hot-plate and pressed her hand right down on to it. Her hand was badly burnt.

Mrs. Burton took immediate action, applying the usual treatment, and binding the hand up, at the same time seeking for the aid of healing for the hand.

We all expected a badly burnt and blistered hand, but when I saw it the next morning, there was no need for any bandages; there were just three red lines where the spirals had made impact across the palm and ball of the thumb. There was not even a blister. Apart from the red lines the hand was clear. There is no doubt that the hand should have been badly burnt but it was not, and there was no pain. It was very clear to us that at the moment of burning, the Spirit doctors were with Edwina and gave her protection.

This is not an isolated story, for I have known other occasions when, with healing, severe burning has had no ill-effects, the flesh being clear of all scarring.

Several years ago we were in Dundee to conduct a healing service and beforehand our friends wished to take us for a car ride to enjoy the beautiful Scottish scenery. After a time, we pulled in to have some tea, and I was the last one to get out of the car.

Before my fingers were clear of the door, however, the driver forcibly slammed it shut. I felt my finger bones crush under the impact and knew, instinctively that my hand had been severely injured. The first thought that flashed into my mind was, "No healing service tonight!"

The driver, who was shocked and alarmed at what had happened immediately flung the door open again, and I pulled my hand clear. I looked at my fingers and was amazed. They looked perfectly normal. Cautiously, I felt the bones and they seemed all right, so I flexed my fingers and could do so without trouble. I had no pain at all. One cannot escape the sensation of feeling one's bones being crushed, as I certainly did, but the healing was instantaneous.

Another personal experience comes to mind; we were travelling by car to Newbury to conduct a healing service, when the car skidded on wet leaves and crashed head-on into a telegraph pole. The car was wrecked.

We were rescued by the wife of a nearby garage proprietor. Mrs. Burton was rather shaken, so it was arranged for her to be taken home while Mr. Burton and I continued on to Newbury in another car.

I did not know it at the time, but I had severely scraped the front of my left leg, taking off the flesh and exposing the bone. I had no pain. We reached Newbury and carried out the healing demonstration as if nothing had happened.

My leg took a while to heal, and the extensive scar tissue which I still have is a testimony to the severity of the wound. I never had any medical attention at the time, and what is remarkable is that I did not experience even one twinge of pain or even aching during the whole time the leg injury was healing over.

In my previous books, I have narrated in full detail the case histories of the phenomenal healings I presented to the Archbishops' Commission on Divine Healing as evidence of spiritual healing. Amongst them were special cases, which I would like to mention briefly here.

One concerned a boy of seven who was in St. Bartholomew's Hospital, London, dying from chronic myeloid leukaemia. Medically, nothing could be done for him and no treatment could be of any avail. The parents were told that their son would die. Within twenty-four hours of absent healing commencing, a change for the better was obvious and before long the boy's blood count was restored to normal. He was sent home, and subsequently went back to school where he played in the school sports. He lived for another nine years. Details connected with his passing are unknown, for strange to say, the parents did not write to me again for healing.

The second case was that of Mr. Olsen, who suffered from spinal collapse. After weeks in hospital, he was finally declared incurable and discharged. His whole body was encased in plaster, even his legs. He could not eat or sleep; the agony was consistent and paralysis was setting in. It was Christmas Eve when Mr. Olsen, in utter desperation, got his wife and son to saw and break off the plaster, and on Christmas morning, he was lifted into a car and brought to me at the Sanctuary. His treatment lasted not more than three minutes. The spinal alignment adjusted, all pain left him, and he was able to walk freely and easily and went home to enjoy his Christmas dinner.

Sometimes people have asked me which case I recall as my "most spectacular cure"—always a very difficult question to answer, especially as I myself, have never "cured" anyone, my part simply being that of a channel for the healing power. However, it may well be, that this next case comes up very high on the list. A boy at the age of three contracted an undiagnosable condition. He could not take food properly, he was just a living skeleton, his condition causing him to sway from side to side. For seven years he was under constant medical attention, being an inmate of various hospitals around Sheffield and later on in the Yarmouth district. He was seen by a host of specialists but all to no avail, finally being brought to London's Great Ormond Street Hospital where he was seen by Mr. Bonham Carter who told the boy's father that nothing could be done for him. The disease was never diagnosed or given a name—it was thought to be a freak condition.

When the boy was taken home at the age of twelve he was a very sad sight. He was by then thinner than ever and the swaying from right to left had become more pronounced. Paralysis had set in and it seemed very clear he would not live for long. It was then that a friend advised the boy's sister to write to me for absent healing. Within three weeks he was eating normally and beginning to put on flesh. The "swaying" ceased, and his recovery made rapid headway and before long he was able to go to school, take part in school sports and pass his G.C.E. examinations. The last I heard was that he was a healthy, upright young man.

The last of these four cases concerns a lady who, for forty years, had been under constant medical treatment with long spells in hospital. Her trouble was chronic kyphosis, her spine being severely wedged, and curved, creating a marked "hunchback" appearance. When she came to the Sanctuary as a last hope, and having no real belief in spiritual healing, she hobbled in on two sticks in very great pain. As in the case of Mr. Olsen, her trouble was removed in a few minutes, the wedging of the spine being overcome, and allowing her to stand upright with a straight back. All pain left her. The free movements for the legs were restored, and she could walk quite comfortably without the need of her sticks. This lady is now a farmer's wife, taking a full part in the farm work, even driving the tractor. In thankfulness for her healing she opened a healing sanctuary of her own.

I am now going to relate the histories of three other cases I submitted to the Archbishops' Commission, giving the comment of the special committee appointed by the British Medical Association in its reports on these cases.

Mr. "B" was suffering from acute pain in the bladder. His local doctor diagnosed this as arising from a wart on the bladder and recommended him to see a specialist. He was admitted into the Royal Masonic Hospital in Brighton, where, following a biopsy, a highly malignant cancerous growth was discovered. An operation was imperative to excise the growth, and it was arranged for this to take place three weeks later.

The day Mr. "B" 's wife received the doctors' verdict she told a friend of the sad news. The friend offered to write to me and did so the same day. I replied to his letter stating that I had commenced absent healing. At no time did I see the patient, and the latter was unaware of the nature of his disease. This, therefore, was the position when spiritual healing commenced: the patient had been diagnosed as suffering from a third degree cancer; it had been pathologically proved, so there was no question here of a "wrong diagnosis"; surgery was necessary if the patient was to have any chance of recovery at all and his condition considered so serious that the specialist advised he should not be told what he was suffering from.

The patient's son became my correspondent and he wrote: "Previously, my father had become very thin in the face, but from the day that Mr. Edwards wrote his appearance was transformed, pain ceased, and he appeared to regain his perfect health. He went to his home in Brighton to recuperate prior to the operation."

During this period the patient had several extremely severe bouts of diarrhoea, but his general condition continued to improve and he put on weight. He duly went into the Royal Masonic Hospital for the operation and when he was opened up, an internal examination showed no trace of cancer whatever and he was sewn up.

The son reported: "The next morning after the operation my father was up and dressed and returned home the following day. Since then he has been in the best of health with no sign of trouble at all."

Mr. "B" had periodical tests at the hospital and on every occasion was declared to be cancer-free.

Some six months later, this same patient became seriously ill with bronchitis and the doctors were doubtful whether he could recover. I received an urgent telephone request for absent healing to be given, and in a very short time his breathing became easier and his chest cleared. He was soon continuing his business.

About three months after this, Mr. "B" suddenly collapsed and died—from a heart attack. The comment of the medical committee, however, was brief and laconic: "The patient died of carcinoma of the bladder."

By virtue of their sacrosanct position, doctors have the last word and nothing is powerful enough to overthrow it. If their verdict in this case is to be accepted after the surgeon, in company with the patient's own two doctors, opened up the patient's bladder and could find no sign of the existence of the cancer which they *knew* to be present from all their previous tests, it implies that they were all suffering from defective eyesight. It also implies that when Mr. "B" had his monthly check-ups at the Royal Masonic Hospital, and being declared to be "cancer free" on every occasion, the doctors concerned were inefficient and did not know what they were talking about.

The British Medical Association's medical committee could have questioned the surgeon and the doctors concerned, but it did not. It could have asked for the patient's medical history; for the biopsy report; of the findings when the patient's bladder was opened for examination; and the medical report when he had his bronchitis and heart condition. This committee did none of these things. To a simple lay-mind like mine, I should have thought that when a man was said to have died from carcinoma of the bladder there would have been some evidence to indicate the presence of cancer in the bladder. The medical committee made no such investigation, finding it far more easy to deny the claim of a spiritual healer in the way it did.

In 1953, a little girl named Susan, living with her parents in Guernsey, found both her thumb-nails had become affected with crusty growths. A little later on her other finger-nails became infected, too.

Her local doctor arranged for her to see the consulting specialist at the Royal South Hampshire Hospital. He confirmed the diagnosis of fungoid growths, and advised that Susan should return to Guernsey and have all her finger-nails taken off. He said this must take place at once and a special lotion be continuously applied.

The specialist said there was no known cure for this infection and was very pessimistic for the future saying, "It is a fungoid growth which is likely to return continuously. The treatment is going to be long, difficult and painful."

The parents told the specialist that as they were in England they were going to take Susan to see Mr. Harry Edwards, the Spiritual Healer in Surrey. The doctor's comment was to the point, for he told them: "Save your money and do not expect a miracle, because you will not get one."

So this was the position the day before Susan was brought to me: the surgical removal of the nails was immediately imperative; there was no known cure; the infection would continue indefinitely and would recur.

In the father's report that he wrote for the Archbishops' Commission, he said: "We were so upset by this news that that same evening I telephoned Mr. Edwards, who kindly consented to see Susan the next morning. Mr. Edwards saw Susan, looked at her

EVIDENTIAL HEALING

hands and held them between his for a while and expressed his willingness to give her absent healing treatment.

"The first clear fact is that the growths, which had been growing then falling off, and then coming again very fast, ceased to show any further activity from the day Mr. Edwards saw Susan.

"On returning to Guernsey, the family doctor decided not to operate until such time as the special lotion became available. The operation to remove the nails was, therefore, delayed for three weeks, after which time it was discovered that the special lotion was no longer being made. A substitute lotion was decided upon, and the doctor informed me that when it arrived he should immediately operate.

"As reported, since we saw Mr. Edwards the condition of the nails had remained stationary, and I thought I could detect a slight improvement. I pointed this out to the doctor and asked if the operation could be postponed.

"The doctor did not agree with me that improvement was visible, but he did agree that the fingers had not worsened. He agreed to postpone operating for two weeks to allow time for any further improvement to show. The substitute lotion had not yet arrived.

"At the end of two weeks the improvement was quite distinct. The doctor was so surprised that he said he would forget the surgery, provided that no relapse occurred.

"The cure continued slowly from week to week. When Susan commenced school in January, the only remaining signs were a distinct roughness on the nails' surface. By the end of March, this year, all fingers were completely normal. There is not the slightest sign today (September) of any trouble or deformity. I do not believe that anyone who saw these fingers ten months ago could possibly have expected them to return to normal shape, no matter how perfect the cure."

The comment of the special medical committee was: "The patient with ringworm of the finger-nails improved but also had medical treatment."

A masterly understatement indeed! For the word "improvement" should have been changed into "totally cured". The doctors did not ask to see Susan, her parents, the specialist or the doctor, or anyone else who could have given them personal evidence on the case. The committee's comment also reminded everyone that Susan had received "medical treatment". The medical treatment was to remove all the nails (which was **not** done) and to apply a special lotion that was not being made any more! This then is the medical treatment with which the **British Medical Association's** committee would have us credit the child's recovery from an incurable condition.

And so we come to the last case in this chapter. It concerns a baby of only five months old whose name is Rosemary. At this age her mother noticed a swelling in the neck and on the advice of her local doctor took the baby to St. John's Hospital, Chelmsford, where a course of injections were given. These did not help and the swelling became larger. At eight months, Rosemary went into this hospital where an operation took place, and after two months, the mother was told that she could take Rosemary home, the dread verdict being that the little one was suffering from a disease for which there was no known cure and the hospital could do nothing further for her.

Rosemary lingered on until she was three and a half years old, when the neck condition again flared up seriously. She was operated upon for the second time by the same surgeon in the same hospital. The surgeon told the mother again that there was no known cure and that Rosemary would die within two years.

The surgeon had the "lumps" he had removed from Rosemary's neck submitted for microscopic examination by a panel of seven expert professors, all of whom were very puzzled. Four of the seven thought it was a kind of cancer, while the remaining three did not; but all agreed it belonged to the family of incurable states.

Rosemary was then taken into a London hospital and placed in the care of two eminent doctors who confirmed the incurable nature of the trouble. At the London hospital she received a course of radiotherapy after which she was sent home "a very sad little child". Once again the mother was told there was no cure and her daughter would die.

It was at this time that a friend asked the parents if she could write to me for absent healing for Rosemary, to which they agreed. From then onward the swellings disappeared and Rosemary's condition steadily improved. She was taken back to the London

EVIDENTIAL HEALING

hospital every month for a check-up, and each time her mother was told that her daughter was well.

The monthly visits were extended to three-monthly ones, and after a year, it was difficult to believe Rosemary was the same child. The hospital Sister actually declared: "This isn't the same child!" At the last visit the mother was told by that doctor that he "could now give Rosemary another year" and hoped by then to discharge her completely.

The same doctor who conducted the microscopical research into the nature of Rosemary's trouble asked to see Rosemary and after giving her an examination told her mother, "I can find nothing at all. She is perfectly well and should go to school." The mother then told this doctor that Rosemary had been receiving spiritual healing from me and his reply was: "All I can say is, this child should not be here." Later on, this interested doctor wrote this letter to Rosemary's mother: "I am very pleased to hear that Rosemary is so well. I think by now you can look forward to her being a perfectly normal child and she should live a perfectly normal life. I can certainly testify that Rosemary is in good health with no apparent signs of new growth."

If we review this case, we find that up to the date of spiritual healing commencing, Rosemary's condition was confirmed by a number of eminent doctors as being hopeless, beyond medical care, and that she would die.

The improvement was dated by the commencement of spiritual healing treatment and progress was rapid and consistent, without any regression.

It may be thought that the original diagnosis that the trouble was cancerous and the opinion of the four professors in thinking so, was wrong, is not necessarily correct. If the growth was cancerous, and removed through spiritual healing, it may well be that the diagnosis was a true one. I have observed many times that doctors have abandoned original diagnoses (sometimes pathologically substantiated) after a change for the better has been brought about by spiritual healing. Doctors therefore mislead themselves by disputing their original diagnosis on the grounds that if it had been correct, their patients could not possibly have got better, and therefore never had the disease in the first place.

Rosemary's cure confounded the prognosis of seven professors, specialists and doctors at the London and Chelmsford hospitals. The nature of her condition was never definitely diagnosed, and medical opinion could offer no curative treatment. Rosemary was scheduled to die.

She has not died and, eighteen years old, she is very well up to the present.

No disease can be intelligently treated unless the precise nature of the trouble can be correctly diagnosed. The weighty medical opinions consulted in this case were unable to give this. As a perfect recovery followed with spiritual healing, it is logical to agree that the spirit doctors were able to diagnose the condition accurately in order to direct to the child the qualitative and particularised healing energies to overcome it.

When I first submitted this case to the Archbishops' Commission, the special British Medical Association committee had not been formed. The commission requested that Rosemary should be examined by a panel of doctors and this was arranged for. Her mother went with her and reports: "The doctors treated her most roughly, with forceful and repeated finger probings all round the neck that frightened Rosemary and made her cry very much. The doctors' only comment was, to bring her back in six months' time."

I am not a doctor, I am only a healer, but it seems to me that such drastic and forceful probing of the neck glands was ill-advised. If the growth had been dormant then this bruising might well have resurrected the trouble. Happily it did not, Rosemary triumphed over this rough handling and is alive and well today.

When the special committee considered this case, its comment was limited to the one word "recovered" with no comment.

It is strange, yet perhaps very eloquent, that after the special committee of doctors made their "official" report on the evidence presented to them, the Archbishops' Commission made the fantastic decision that to investigate evidence in support of spiritual healing was outside its "terms of reference". Surely nothing could be more contrary. One is entitled to wonder what the "unofficial" commentary was, to induce both Church and Medicine to turn their backs upon the obvious job they had to do.

CHAPTER FIFTEEN

A DOCTOR TESTIFIES

DR. Mahmoud K. Muftic, B.Sc., M.D. is a doctor engaged on medical research at the Institute for Experimental Medicine, in the Medical Teaching Hospital at Borstel, Ded Oldesloe, in Western Germany.

There have been a number of occasions when I have submitted case histories with evidence for super-normal recoveries for medical scrutiny and comment. Generally these have been treated evasively. In the healing story that follows, a doctor engaged in medical research provides his own case history and commentary—not for another patient but for himself.

He is a doctor with vision and has sought for some degree of association between the medical profession and healers. He came to the United Kingdom with the purpose of receiving healing for himself and to see to what extent such co-operation could be established. After his visit he wrote the following report for me:

"A few years ago I asked Mr. Harry Edwards to organise a proper scientific control of the cases which requested his help. This would, of course, entail a clinic where each case could be examined and staffed by trained technical people, physicians, radiologists and pathologists.

"In addition to the fact that this would require a great amount of financial support, it is probable that the medical people collaborating would have found themselves in danger of being struck off the Register, and prevented by the British Medical Council of examining patients and providing official reports. It was only last year, during my visit to England, that I learned of these facts.

"Before I came to England I suffered from serious stomach troubles. Excessive pain, with alternating heartburn and acute acidity, obliged me to be radiologically examined. Severe chronic gastritis with hypersecretion, and two small ulcers, one at a major and one at a minor site, were discovered. After blood analysis, a diagnosis of pancreatitis was given.

"It was difficult to support the pain without strong analgesics and a high dosage of belladonna, and twice I suffered haematemesis losing about half a pint of blood. One of my ulcers was penetrated, and only surgical intervention saved my life. All investigations were carried out in Hamburg University clinics and there was no doubt about any dissimulate diagnosis.

"It is interesting to note that the last year research project in our laboratories was pancreatitis and other autolytic processes, where we tested new "bayer" drugs used in the palliative treatment of the affection. Mortality in this field is very high and a practical cure never reached.

"Before I came to Harry Edwards I was fighting every day, every hour, as I was unable to get any further relief from drugs or by diet. My desire for life became subservient to the desire to get rid of pain and suffering.

"I was with Mr. Edwards for a short contact healing, not exceeding ten minutes, and following this I had no more pain. I investigated my blood in Paddington Hospital with Dr. Beck and my blood analysis was normal. Later I had radiological investigations in England and Germany. There was no more gastritis, no more atonia in duodenal ulcers. What happened?

"What caused the ulcers to disappear? Was the earlier diagnosis an illusion? Were all my sufferings, the bleeding, the impossible pain, illusions? All these questions belong to the critical human mind and deserve full consideration. I was suffering intensely—now I am free of pain.

"If Mr. Edwards effected this relief by psychological means, either in suppressing an imaginary disease or suppressing my realisation of real disease, I will say that every physician should be proud of themselves if they afford only a partial relief to my sufferings as was done by Mr. Edwards to me.

"Time has passed, and I am living without pain, eating normal food, sometimes with heavy spices. I have no more heartburn, no more acidity. There is none of the usual "hunger-pain" even if I take my lunch ten hours after breakfast. I would be extremely happy if such "illusions" could be effected by my colleagues, or even by myself, to my patients.

'But we are still very far from this realisation because nobody appears to try to study this phenomena, even from the most sceptical angle.

"I wish Harry Edwards a long and fruitful life, but like every other human, one day he will be no longer living. I am sure we will regret not having taken advantage of this wonderful opportunity to study the phenomena of spiritual healing under such a successful exponent of this form of healing.

"I am not intending to praise Mr. Edwards; I am sure he is against such things. But my consciousness as a physician and scientist on one part, and as a grateful patient on the other, to publish these few words as a testimony of what I have experienced.

"It is a pity that British scientific investigation is not alive to the benefits which could ensue from the examination of facts as they are. Mr. Edwards is the forerunner of an era which is coming now."

CHAPTER SIXTEEN

SPIRITUAL HEALING AND CHILDBIRTH

WE are often asked to help mothers expecting babies, especially when a difficult birth is expected. Usually, with healing, the baby arrives normally and without undue stress.

We know how beneficial healing can be in soothing fears, anxieties, tensions and frustrations and how by good influencing and direction, muscular spasms, contractions, and cramps can be eased. It may well be that healing influencing reaches the mother at the time of delivery, enabling her to co-operate with the muscular actions and processes which induce a normal birth.

Furthermore, when the mother knows she is receiving absent healing, giving her the expectation of a delivery free from stress and complications, it does much to overcome the mother's fears and help her to co-operate with the functions of birth.

I recall the case of a friend in her mid-forties who was having her first baby. A hazardous time was expected, and as a safety precaution she was admitted into hospital four weeks before the baby was due so that she could be kept under constant observation by the doctors.

As the time drew near for the baby's arrival, the doctor was keeping her under very close observation and everything was prepared for all the emergency aids to be ready. The woman duly commenced her labour and was moved into a special labour room. She was certainly not over-stressed and so confident was the nurse in charge of her, that she went out of the room for a few moments to see to something. Whilst her patient was in the toilet, and before the woman could get back to the couch, a baby boy was born. It was as simple as that. A year or so later the mother gave birth to a daughter without any trouble.

A second case concerns a woman who lived in Surbiton. She

had had one child, but the birth was extremely difficult with severe complications that endangered her life. The doctors told her she should avoid having another baby; but things did not work out that way, and a second baby was on its way.

The woman, her husband, and parents were greatly worried. They were all believers in spiritual healing and sought our aid, keeping us constantly informed and we saw the patient personally as well.

It was arranged that the birth should take place in Kingston Hospital and a specialist in gynaecology from St. Thomas's Hospital in London should come down to Kingston as soon as labour commenced.

The day arrived when the early signs of labour became noticeable. The gynaecologist was telephoned for and was said to be on his way, meanwhile the mother and her daughter went to Kingston Hospital. Upon arrival, it was found that the private room booked was not quite ready and they were requested to stay in a waiting-room. It was while they were waiting there that the baby "slipped out" with no tension, labour pains or other discomfort.

Finally I would like to tell about another mother who had already given birth to two children, each time the birth being extremely difficult, with long labour and much pain. She dreaded the ordeal with great fear.

Upon conceiving again, she wrote to me telling about her previous stressful confinements and how she dreaded the coming ordeal, saying she would rather die than have another baby. We sought through absent healing to comfort her in the months before the baby was due, and I arranged for her to let me know when the baby's arrival was imminent. She did so, and special help was sought for her. Coincidence or not, her third baby arrived exceedingly easy; there was a very short and comparatively painless labour, and the little one emerged without any stress or need for stitches, etc.

The Healing of Children

Some of the most difficult cases healers are asked to help are those of children who are both physically and mentally retarded. I have already referred to instances of healing spastic children, but the tragic little lives who are mentally dumb present an even greater challenge.

Generally speaking, they are "written off" by the doctors and considered to be beyond all human help; indeed, it is thought to try and bring about a livening of the mental faculties is a waste of doctors' time.

In some cases it appears that the child has not even the intelligence of an animal, like a dog, horse or cat. Such children are untrainable and incapable of appreciating right from wrong, possessing no conscience at all.

It is not possible to give a percentage of healing in these cases. Oft-times the child is brought to the Sanctuary or, alternatively, receives absent healing. We recognise that when spiritual healing can intervene it will take time before some degree of normality is brought about. This entails constant and patient encouragement by the parents and the healer who does not usually lose patience, but it is more understandable that the parents who have to "endure" the child day by day, may, and therefore discontinue to maintain association with the healer.

It would be very wrong of me to imply any blame to the parents who may lose interest and submit their child to an institution. The mother's health may rightly be the primary consideration, and I have been impressed over and over again with the wonderful love and patience parents give to an afflicted child.

It is my opinion that these children need, in addition to spiritual healing, the intelligent, encouraging love with understanding of the parents to nurture all signs of improvement even though they may seem negligible at first.

We have found that there are certain characteristics common to these children. They are unusually affectionate, they love to receive physical affection, and to be cuddled and soothed. They are attracted to, and follow closely music of the rhythmic sort. They like to make a noise and to tear up paper, or play with water, etc. If the parent builds up a wall of toy blocks, they love to knock it down. These are some of the factors that can be used in awakening the co-ordination of thought. It is not my purpose here to go into detail with the various modes of treatment we suggest for parents to co-operate with the healing influences to awaken the dormant mind to constructive thought; to teach the child body discipline; to awaken anticipation of events, and to associate one form of thought with another. I can say this, that when we have co-operative parents, we observe measureable degrees of progress, commencing in very small ways at first, but from the small beginnings, progress is more and more marked. The association of sound with objects, the encouragement of speaking words to describe them, the recognition of things with sounds and words, and so on, are all part of the healing process in which parental co-operation is essential.

Suffice it, therefore, that in numbers of cases, we have seen children approach or reach normality, who otherwise would have remained mentally inert.

CHAPTER SEVENTEEN

THE HEALING OF A SCULPTOR'S LIMBS

Written by Dick Tatham

It had been there ever since he could remember—the physical disablement that made him so different from other people. . . . Even as a small boy he had quickly come to realise that outdoor games and general scampering around were not for him. His limbs just would not function the way he wanted. Try, as he would, he could move around with only a laboured gait. Often there was bodily pain from the swollen misplaced knee and elbow joints. And there was pain of mind: the hurtful awareness that he was cut off from the fun and comradeship of other boys of his age; the feeling that, wherever he went, people were staring at him.

But, in fact, people hardly ever stared at him—not those kindly folk who lived near his home in Lucerne, Switzerland. When little Rudi Limacher came by, they would make no reference to his deformity—unless, of course, he brought the subject up himself. Then they would say: "Let us hope that one day you will be better. You are seeing the doctor again one day soon? Good! Maybe he will find some way . . ."

But the years went by and still no solution was found. As Rudi grew to early manhood a fresh challenge awaited him—that of earning a living. No matter how severe and restricting his bodily ailment might be, he told himself that if he could make himself financially independent, at least that would make him mentally stronger. To be dependent on others all the time was unthinkable to him.

The solution came to him gradually. At first he dared hardly hope that this could be the key to his independence. It was his carving. He had grown up with a gift for it. Despite the stiffness in his joints, despite the fact that his fingers lacked the natural suppleness given to others, he found he could fashion models of all kinds.

His plan worked. The demand for his wood and stone carvings grew from a fitful start to a steady flow of orders. At first people wanted something made to decorate their homes or gardens. Then, with Rudi's reputation spreading far beyond Lucerne, big firms began to commission him whenever a job needed special expertness. Finally churches started commissioning his exquisite wood carvings. So in this way, Rudi Limacher overcame his handicap—but he never ceased to hope that one day it might disappear altogether.

Many years went by without improvement and he was past his fortieth birthday when for the first time he heard of spiritual healer Harry Edwards.

Friends of his who had visited Britain came back with news of the healer's achievements. And as he listened, Rudi became convinced that somehow he must visit Britain himself and try to see Harry Edwards. It was some months before he could do so. For one thing, business commitments were heavy. For another, he spoke no English. But by the summer of 1962 he was all set for the trip. He would take a holiday in Britain and hope to arrange to see Harry Edwards while he was there.

Then through friends he was fortunate enough to make contact with someone who was willing to help him. A Mrs. Unden, widow of a professor of languages, who was fluent in German, Rudi's native language. She met him at the airport with the wonderful news that she had already been in touch with Harry Edwards at Burrows Lea, and that an appointment had been made for the following Thursday afternoon.

I was present at the healing session which Rudi Limacher attended, and I watched him come slowly forward, haltingly, with a troubled gait, supporting his movements with the aid of a stick.

George Burton, Harry Edwards's colleague, placed a steadying hand on his elbow and guided him towards the stool opposite the chair on which Mr. Edwards was seated.

At the same time, silver-haired Mrs. Unden came forward....
"I'm afraid Mr. Limacher speaks no English," she explained. "But I will translate everything as quickly as possible."

"Please sit down," Harry Edwards replied, motioning towards a chair to one side of him.

Then he added: "First of all would you kindly ask him to relax. I know it may be difficult as he is in strange surroundings. But it helps the treatment if the patient is relaxed."

The sculptor smiled and nodded when the request was translated, and soon lost the signs of tension he had shown on coming forward. He seemed reasonably composed as Harry Edwards took his right arm and started gently to flex it.

But it was obvious there was little "give" in the arm. Then Mr. Edwards began to manipulate the patient's right elbow. He worked with firm, purposeful motions till one could see it was gaining greater freedom of movement, and the kinking of the elbow lessened as the arm became straight. Then he concentrated in similar fashion on the shoulder joint until that was swinging loosely.

"Now, please tell him to move his arm slowly himself . . ."

Cautiously the sculptor did so. His movements gathered energy, until he was working his right arm to and fro against the pressure of Edwards's left.

"Now ask him to raise his arm above his head. . . ."

Rudi looked hesitant when the suggestion was translated, and there were signs of tension returning.

"Tell him not to worry. Tell him to raise his arm slowly . . . slowly. . . ."

Then, despite the disbelief, written on his features, Rudi gradually raised his arm. Slowly, up and up it went until it was at full stretch above his head.

"Please ask him when he was last able to do that . . ."

The sculptor did not need words to answer Mr. Edwards's question. He merely gave a smile and placed his hand about three feet from the floor. He had been a small boy when he was last able to lift his hands aloft.

Methodically, Harry Edwards set about treating his other limbs. His was a dual task, since he had both to concentrate on manipulating the locked joints and, at the same time, to counter the mental stress which built up from time to time in the patient. To be asked to make movements he had not carried out for years naturally called for an effort of mind as well as body.

THE HEALING OF A SCULPTOR'S LIMBS

"Please tell him again to relax . . . to make his effort slowly . . . to rest assured I shall not hurt him in any way. . . ."

The arms, the fingers, the legs . . . When at last Harry Edwards had worked on them all, making each flexible, he motioned to the sculptor to stand. At the same time he nodded to George Burton, who placed his hand lightly on the patient's elbow.

This time Rudi, without his stick, began to walk across the floor of the hushed Sanctuary.

"Tell him to walk steadily . . . Tell him not to try and walk fast and jerkily . . . but slowly and smoothly . . . lifting his knees up for each step, and using his feet flexibly. . . ."

"It's unbelievable!"

The exclamation came spontaneously from Mrs. Unden, as she saw the normal way in which the Swiss was moving.

Harry Edwards smiled.

"This should be the start of a new chapter for him," he told her. "An important part of taking advantage of the healing is to work through his mind. We have seen how well he can respond. But we have to impress upon him how essential it is for him to give his limbs time to react. He must, for the time being, discipline himself to make slow but controlled movements, instead of hasty, jerky ones."

Over tea, after the healing session was over, I found the sculptor and his friend full of optimism. "The results Mr. Edwards has brought about this afternoon are remarkable," said Mrs. Unden.

A few minutes later Mr. Edwards joined us.

Turning to Mrs. Unden, he said: "Please encourage Mr. Limacher to maintain his normal movements, like everyone else. He must conquer the habit of his past ways, and to move his limbs in the way I have shown him, until he adopts naturally the new habit of correct movement."

As Mrs. Unden translated, Rudi Limacher nodded cheerfully. "Tell Mr. Edwards I will do that and keep in regular touch with him."

And judging by the look of fresh hope in his eyes, it was obvious he felt the long journey to see Harry Edwards had been well worth while.

CHAPTER EIGHTEEN

PUBLIC HEALING DEMONSTRATIONS

In the years gone by, when we conducted public healing services in the largest halls our main cities possessed, we would need to have a long Press table and accustom ourselves to the flashlights of a battery of Press cameras. The services were reported in both local and national newspapers, but as time went on, and each report told similar stories of outstanding recoveries so they ceased to be "news". Editors would say: "We have printed all that before." A repetition of "miracles"—a word used frequently in Press reports, not mine—can become boring.

We have filled the Royal Albert Hall on several occasions and the Royal Festival Hall annually. In Scotland, the great halls in Edinburgh, Glasgow, Dundee and Aberdeen have not been large enough to accommodate all who wished to attend, all tickets having been disposed of weeks before the date of the service.

My mind goes back to the largest gathering we have ever held, when seven thousand people filled the King's Hall, Bellevue, in Manchester. At this meeting in addition to the host of reporters and camera men, a film unit made a film with the floodlights bearing hotly upon us.

These services are conducted reverently as a religious service. While the healing of the sick is always somewhat emotional there has never been any hysteria.

The procedure on these occasions is that I ask for patients suffering from specified diseases to hold up their hands and I choose, at random, one from the left side of the hall and another from the right or from the balconies. No previous arrangements are ever made to see any particular person.

We have to discriminate in the kind of diseases selected. It is obvious that we could not demonstrate with, say, diabetes or

PUBLIC HEALING DEMONSTRATIONS

apoplexy or other complaints which would need a period of time to prove the fulfilment of the healing. Therefore we suggest such diseases as acute rheumatoid arthritis, spinal lesions, curvatures and forms of paralysis (like disseminated sclerosis), emphysema, blindness, deafness, etc., so that noticeable improvements can be made obvious to the audience.

The patients so selected are aided to the platform, sometimes carried or assisted up the steps to the platform level. Healer stewards render this service or it is undertaken by the St. John Ambulance Brigade, who invariably are in attendance on these occasions.

The patient is seated before me and by questioning I get the medical history; how long he has suffered; what hospitals he has attended; the medical opinion about his condition today; what treatment, if any, he is receiving. This information is passed on to the audience so that they, too, can have a picture of the patient's condition before healing commences. Sometimes patients tell their story direct over the microphone.

Generally it is a tragic story, telling of suffering and pain over a good number of years and the final verdict that the doctors can do no more for them, other than prescribe pain-killing tablets. In the field of healing, a sufferer will be brought to the platform with deep-seated and chronic infirmities. The healing takes place and nothing more is heard for a long time and then, years later, comes the tribute that the healing has been absolute, as the writer will testify upon writing for healing for someone else.

Spiritual healing is not omnipotent, it can only take place within the total laws that govern life; but within the scope of those laws much can be done. Sometimes it happens (happily only rarely) that having chosen a patient from the audience it becomes obvious that as he is being led or carried from the body of the hall on to the platform, the nature and severity of the affliction would make it appear to be quite beyond the "scheme of things" for relief to be demonstrated, such as with acute spondylitis or the ill-effects arising from surgery.

Such was a case treated at the Royal Albert Hall where a service was being held in protest over the report issued by the Archbishops' Commission on Divine Healing. We were profoundly disappointed with this. Very strangely the Commission had ruled that all evidence testifying to spiritual healing was outside its "terms of reference". This Royal Albert Hall service was held in protest.

Before a capacity audience we brought forward a number of the patients whose cases we had submitted to the Commission to tell publicly, and demonstrate, their recoveries from so-called "incurability". These cases are mentioned in Chapter Thirteen. The latter half of the service was devoted to a demonstration of healing of the sick who were present, and as the meeting drew to a close, the last patient was brought to the platform.

He had not been chosen by me, in the usual way, but was brought on to the platform by some well-intentioned, but overzealous stewards. Apparently, a lady on her way to the service, saw a man selling matches in the street and her compassion for him was so aroused, that she took a chance and brought him along to the hall.

As he was brought on to the platform he looked a pitiful sight, and when I saw the terrible condition he was in, my heart sank for a moment or two, for my reasoning mind placed him in the category of those for whom no measurable improvement could possibly be anticipated. As he was the last patient, the prospect of a good termination to the demonstration seemed remote. The man was on the platform before me and I could do nothing else but see what the power of healing could do for him.

The patient was using a white stick and was nearly blind. His slow, faltering, shuffling steps indicated advanced paralysis. He was bent over and woefully thin, his face haggard from suffering and malnutrition.

The lady who had brought him to the service was rewarded, for in the healing that followed, she saw his curved back straighten up, his legs given new strength as he "goose-walked" across the platform and go down the steps unaided; but perhaps the greatest change took place in his sight, for this cleared and he was intensely happy.

His good samaritan lady watched over him for some weeks afterwards and she kept me informed about him. His improvements were maintained; his outlook on life became cheerful and uplifted and he was able to obtain light-employment.

One can go on telling of healings at these public demonstrations but they tend to become tedious, so I will be content with just one

PUBLIC HEALING DEMONSTRATIONS

more illustration of a healing that occurred at the Royal Festival Hall.

On the morning of the Royal Festival Hall service, a man who was seventy-one years of age, startled his wife by telling her "I am going out, trust me, but do not ask any questions." The man's name is Mr. Searle, and he lived in Gillingham, Kent. For years he had suffered from osteo and rheumatoid arthritis, his right leg was shrunken, the hip was permanently stiff and he could only get about with the use of sticks. He was one of those chosen from the audience for treatment, so his faith and courage in making the journey from Gillingham to London by himself, sadly handicapped as he was, was rewarded.

He had to be assisted on to the platform, and in my questioning to give the audience a picture of his condition, it was revealed that he had been suffering for five years, and had had surgery on his hip, which had stiffened the joint and made it immobile. He had been given radiotherapy and sedation medicines but the pain and immovability of the hip remained.

The knee too was fixed and incapable of bending. First of all, healing was directed to his arthritically fixed spine. This was soon freed. At first the back moved just a little backwards and forwards, then the mobility increased, and he was able to swing his body sideways, and pivot the spine.

When I commenced to treat the hip, it was apparent that the surgery had immobilised it, and I told the audience that we may not see any marked improvement; but it came, responding so well that the leg could be lifted up.

I then said I would try to get the knee to bend. Mr. Searle commented, "Well, it will be a miracle," and he added, "his wife had always had to put on his sock and shoe for him."

The "miracle" took place. A minute later he could bring his right knee up to waist level and without any pain.

Overcome with emotion, Mr. Searle could only say: "Excuse me while I blow my nose," and he brushed away his tears of relief.

Loud applause echoed through the huge hall as Mr. Searle briskly marched off the platform. He exaggerated his leg movements, to demonstrate to the audience how well the healing had made him free.

It was at this point that I noticed his sticks lying idle on the platform. I passed them to Mr. Searle who triumphantly held them head high.

After the meeting a Press reporter questioned him and was shown his new ability to move his leg. For instance he sat down into his seat and said: "There I couldn't do that before, I had to put my leg out straight into the aisle because I could not bend it." He stood up and down again repeatedly to prove he had no pain, and the reporter described this in his Press report.

I often wondered what his wife said when eventually Mr. Searle returned home, for he had told the reporter, "She doesn't attach much importance to spirit healing."

The photograph (plate 7) showing the healing of arthritic hands is typical. In the inset circles the knotted and distorted fingers are shown before the healing was given. In the main picture the hands are seen nearly normal, and the sufferer is able to grasp my hand firmly and shake it without pain.

Such arthritic hands are terribly painful, but it is our general experience that after healing the patient is able to really grip my hand and pull it strongly without even a twinge of discomfort.

The happy lady photographed at her kitchen stove (plate 6) is a further testimony to the healing of arthritis. This healing took place in Southampton at a Healing Service organised by *Psychic News* and the *Sunday Citizen*. The transformation is not only seen with the removal of the arthritis but in the removal of the stress lines of pain on the face showing a return of happiness and health. A similar transformation is observed on the picture of the blind and crippled man healed at The Royal Albert Hall (plate 4). In the top picture the anguished face is seen as the man tells the audience his medical history. Then after Olive Burton has given him back the power to see, the transformation in the face is obvious as he cracks a joke with me.

It is a general characteristic, with healing, by both the personal and absent healing methods that patients become conscious of a sense of inner upliftment and happiness. This is only natural for both the cause and symptoms have been relieved.

CHAPTER NINETEEN

"I THOUGHT I'D NEVER KNIT AGAIN"

FOR the past twelve years, *True Magazine* has featured the work of the Sanctuary in every monthly issue. For a national magazine to sustain a series for so long is not only unusual, but pays a high compliment to spiritual healing for the editorial staff to consider it worth while. As I write now, the series is continuing.

Sometimes the editor has sent a special reporter to visit some of our patients in person and to get their story at first hand, and one of these is well worth recounting:

"It started with her left hand. . . . She remembers waking one morning to find it swollen and discoloured. . . . She recalls the pain and also the puzzlement, for there had been no sign of anything wrong the night before. There was the period of trying to carry on despite it—of hoping the swelling would go down and the pain disappear. Then the gradual facing of the fact that she just *couldn't* carry on—that something *had* to be done.

"Mrs. Ferdinando is a typical homely, hardworking mother of an ordinary, average family. She lives in Chesterfield Road, Leyton.

"You will find hundreds of such streets in East London. And you will find thousands of housewives, such as Mrs. Ferdinando—caught up in the day-to-day struggle of raising children, of managing on a modest budget, of having a warm and cheerful home for a husband to return to from work each evening. Probably she has more to cope with than most women in her walk of life, for she has five children. Certainly this made things all the more acute for her that morning late in 1961 when she woke to find her hand so severely swollen.

" 'I was in an immediate fix with little Christine, my youngest. She was then still in the nappie stage, and I realised that I wouldn't be able to put them on and take them off properly, let alone be able to keep them laundered.

"'I found, for example, I couldn't do my hair. And it was practically impossible to do ordinary things, like making a bed or shaking a mat. But I never went short of help for my good neighbours came to my rescue, over and over again.

"'Meantime, of course, I had gone to see the doctor. He promptly sent me to the local hospital. I wasted no time getting there, for I believed they would soon get to the root of the trouble, and that I would soon be running the home myself once more instead of having to trouble the neighbours.

"'My hand had become so swollen that they had to cut through my wedding ring to get it off. At first it seemed I must have broken a bone in my hand; but then the X-rays showed this wasn't so. I was told I would have to come in regularly for treatment, though they couldn't say how long it might take to put things right. With a husband and five lively children to look after, I just hoped and prayed the trouble would not last long. . . .'

"When we hope intensely for things to get better it is always a bitter moment when we suddenly realise they are, in fact, getting worse. Such a moment was to come to Mrs. Ferdinando. She continues her story:

"'The pain and the stiffness began to work upwards. My left arm began to be affected. Then my shoulders and neck. Then my right arm. Now I could not even attempt to do my hair—I simply wasn't able to reach upwards.

"'I did my best to help about the house; but I could hardly even pick anything up and hold it. I began dropping things.

"'Another thing—I loved to knit. It always relaxes me and takes my mind off problems. Now I found I could not even hold the needles!

"'Then, to add to the family difficulties, my husband became ill. Last year he had to go into hospital for a lung operation. I knew that when he came out it would be months before he would be able to start work as a french polisher again. And still there was no sign of the stiffness in the top part of my body disappearing. I was getting desperate; I didn't know what to do. . . .'

"Then, completely unexpectedly, came a gleam of hope. Mrs. Ferdinando hardly dared to believe it might be a way out.

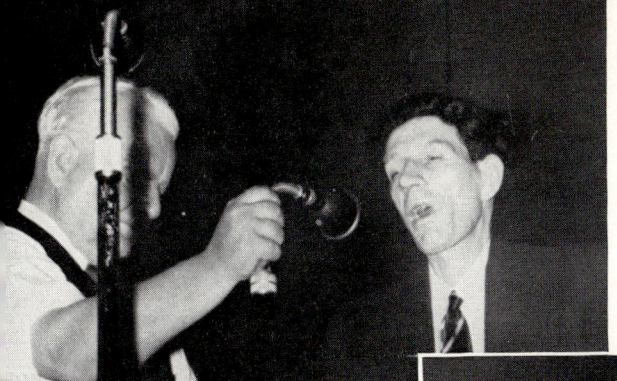

Left: The patient tells his story before an Albert Hall audience. He is crippled and almost blind

Right: Olive Burton gives healing for the eyes, restoring the sight

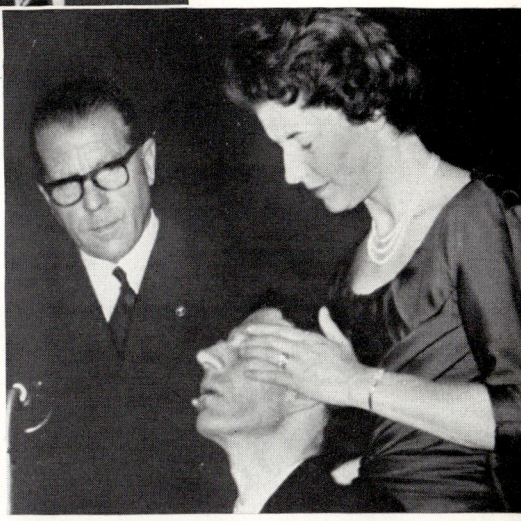

Above: A joke after the healing causes smiles all round

Right: The patient is able to walk normally and can see well again. Note the two sticks (one white) being held by Harry Edwards

Above: A lady suffering from chronic arthritis is painfully helped to the platform to receive healing, prior to which she could not stand without the support of her two walking sticks

Below: The lady in her home a few days later. Freed from pain, she can now move around without her sticks. Her finger joints, too, are now unlocked

" 'Some relatives who had a car came to see me one day,' she recalls. 'They said they were going down to Southend the following Tuesday and thought I might like to go with them, bringing a couple of the children. I jumped at the chance of some sea air and a day away from everything. They called for me as arranged, and we had not been long started on the journey when they told me there were some magazines in the door pocket if I felt like reading. It was just as well I did feel like reading, for *True Magazine* was one of the publications, and by the time we were half-way to Southend I had become deeply interested in an article about Harry Edwards.

" 'As I read, the question naturally started to build up in my mind: Could he do anything to help me? I spoke to my relatives about it. Also, after I had got back to Chesterfield Road, I discussed the matter with several friends. To be honest, quite a few of them said it would be a waste of time, that there must be a catch in it.

" 'Then I remembered there was a lady living a couple of streets away who was interested in spiritual healing. She had often spoken to me about it, but frankly I had never been convinced that there was anything in it. Just the same, I called round to see her. She told me, "I think there is every chance you will receive help, but in any case what is there to lose by trying?" There was no denying that: I had nothing to lose!'

"Then came the day when she wrote to Mr. Edwards, giving an outline of her trouble. She recalls her difficulty in writing the letter: 'If I had been left-handed I should have had to get someone to write it for me.' Then after a day or two, the reply. She had been chosen as one of a party of patients to visit Burrows Lea on a trip organised by *True Magazine*.

" 'I was so terribly nervous! That may sound silly, seeing that I was going to someone who would obviously be all out to help me, but nevertheless it was how I felt. On the train to Guildford, I kept wondering what Harry Edwards would be like, and what kind of treatment he would give me.

" 'I felt a bit more at ease when I joined the rest of the party in the coach which was waiting at Guildford station to take us the rest of the way—they all seemed ordinary, friendly people. The lovely country we drove through from Guildford to Burrows Lea helped to relax me, too.'

"The few minutes of waiting as Mrs. Ferdinando and the other patients sat quietly in the Sanctuary at Burrows Lea.... Then all eyes turning to the door as Harry Edwards came in with his helpers, George and Olive Burton, and Ray and Joan Branch.

" 'There is something about Mr. Edwards', Mrs. Ferdinando says, 'that makes you feel at ease immediately. He is so frank and cheerful. When my turn came to sit in front of him, he spoke in such a natural, friendly way. He asked me a few questions, then he started to clear away the stiffness....'

"I was present at that healing session. I recall clearly how the strong, square hands of Harry Edwards began to work on the afflicted hands of Mrs. Ferdinando—and how results showed almost at once as she flexed her fingers more and more freely. Then came her arms, shoulders and neck and the loosening process went steadily on. At last, Harry Edwards urged her, 'Now move your hands right up to your head, as if you were about to do your hair....'

"She hesitated for a moment, as if in disbelief, then she tried—and succeeded! 'I haven't been able to do that for months!' she said, wonderingly.

" 'Keep in touch. Let us know how things go. But I think you will be all right from now on,' Harry Edwards told her.

"It was some four months later that I called to see Mrs. Ferdinando at her home.

" 'The trouble has gone completely,' she assured me. Nods of agreement came from her children—Michael (fifteen), Derek (twelve), Peter (ten), Linda (seven), and little Christine, now aged two.

" 'Yes,' she went on, 'I'm back to normal with my housework. I can do laundry, wash-up, make the beds, fix my hair—all as I did before the trouble started.'

" 'And the knitting?' I asked.

"Chuckles came from the boys. Then I noticed they were wearing bright, new jerseys. I heard Mrs. Ferdinando say: 'Yes: I made those. Since I visited Mr. Edwards, I've knitted six jerseys for the boys and a cardigan for Linda. And I confess there was a time when I thought I'd never be able to pick up my needles again....' "

CHAPTER TWENTY

MY DREAM CAME TRUE AT LAST

By Carol Robinson

My trouble started when I was sixteen years old, when it was first diagnosed that I had curvature of the spine. My doctor sent me to hospital where I was fitted with a support for my spine.

I was encased in it from neck to thigh.

Each week, when I went for a check-up, the jacket and the additional leg splints were adjusted more tightly to my body.

In hot weather, my "harness", as I called it was unendurable. Each night I would go to bed early; just to be free from the constriction. It seemed to imprison not only my body but my spirit too . . . which put me apart from others, made me unable to earn a living.

Then, one summer's day, suddenly I could submit no longer!

Seeing an advertisement in the local paper for a Mother's Help, I took off my harness and went out to apply for the job. I got it—at a salary of seven and sixpence a week, all found.

But when I told my mother the news, she did not see things from my viewpoint! "Carol, you're not fit to work," she cried. "You must get well before you can go out into the world."

"No!" Rebelliously I faced her. "I refuse to wear that contraption any more! I'm going to forget my spine trouble. I'm going to lead a useful life." I burst into tears. "I'm finished with doctors and hospitals!" I cried defiantly.

In vain my parents and the family doctor persuaded me to try further treatment for my deformed spine. I would not listen. I was deaf to everything but that voice inside me telling me to go out and live.

The voice, of course, deceived me. I realise now, with the

wisdom of fifty-six years, that I made a mistake in being so headstrong. It would have been braver to try curing my spinal condition instead of ignoring it. But once set upon my path of independence I would not digress. From being a Mother's Help I moved to more strenuous jobs. I worked hard. Too hard.

By the time I was twenty-one my spine was weaker than ever. Moreover, this basic trouble had affected my chest, too. I started getting frequent colds and bronchitis.

At last I was forced to seek medical treatment. At the hospital they told me, 'You will notice your health condition more as you get older. Don't try to undertake too much."

I ignored these ominous words. Between long spells in bed with bronchitis and pneumonia, I tried for better and better jobs. And in 1957 I found a really good clerical position with prospects.

"I've beaten the doctors," I triumphantly told friends. "There's nothing much wrong with me! I'll be able to carry on and save up for my old age."

Watching their unresponsive faces, I knew my words did not delude them. And I could not delude myself either. With my stiff back, stiff limbs, numb fingers; with my ever-worsening bronchial trouble, I realised that despite my optimism and my will-power, my health was declining.

At the age of fifty-two, after a severe attack of pneumonia, it seemed I had lost my battle. From that time on I was unable to work. Through enforced idleness my strength and energy, my lung capacity, grew even less. Yet still a voice within me kept telling me not to give in, not to accept my beating.

Then, a year ago, I read about Mr. Edwards and his work at Burrows Lea. At last I knew I had found a logical backing for my optimism.

The idea of spiritual healing—the help that Mr. Harry Edwards could give me through his special healing powers in which faith and prayer play so much part—tuned in with my own unexpressed ideas. With a patient like me, who had always refused to give in to fate, surely Mr. Edwards would have success.

So I wrote to Mr. Edwards for an appointment which he kindly arranged.

With kindliness and confidence, the keen blue eyes of Spiritual Healer, Harry Edwards quickly appraised me.

MY DREAM CAME TRUE AT LAST

"Sit on this stool," he said. "Tell me about your trouble."

Briefly, I gave him a summary of my medical history; the curvature of the spine, the bronchial attacks which had plagued my life. In the soothing peace of his Sanctuary, Mr. Edwards listened. Then he placed strong, firm hands on my back. With cheerful words of encouragement he bent my body backwards and forwards. He rotated my knee and my ankle. Under his touch I felt taut muscles relax, my stiff joints moved with unaccustomed ease and suppleness.

Then he massaged my hands. My fingers were usually numb, but now I felt them as a living part of me. Next came the breathing treatment.

"Breathe in . . . out . . . breathe through your nose . . . open your lungs and let your chest expand. Look for this and encourage it with every slow deep indrawn breath." His eyes closed in concentration, so Mr. Edwards instructed me. And, as gently, he placed his hands on my shoulders, the heaviness in my chest seemed to vanish. I was able to do as he said . . . breathe deeply, smoothly.

As the next patient approached the healer, I returned to my seat filled with an inexplicable sense of uplift and well-being. For the first time since childhood, I could stand erect with a straight spine and my limbs felt loose and free. Already I felt healthier, happier.

Now that the time has come, I will be truthful. I will not exaggerate.

Since my visit to Mr. Edwards, though my spine is not completely straight, a great improvement has taken place, I am more upright, and I move much more freely. As for my chest condition, I did have but one bronchial spell this winter, it only lasted three days. Right now I feel so fit I am again seeking a job—some light clerical position which will not prove beyond my physical capacity.

Meantime I write weekly to Mr. Edwards about my health, knowing that his prayers and concentration of his powers are still with me . . . giving me strength and well-founded hope of even better health.

CHAPTER TWENTY-ONE

SPIRITUAL HEALING CAN MISLEAD DOCTORS

I AM informed that at an Annual Meeting of the British Medical Association held in the South of England, the doctors assembled were able to see on closed circuit television five cases of supernormal healings that were incomprehensible to medical science.

These five cases were chosen because of the unusual pattern of the recoveries. They were all of "incurable diseases" for which there was no known effective medical treatment. They were said to be "spontaneous healings", and they were selected for demonstration because they were so unusual.

Now, what the doctors responsible for this programme did not know, was that three of the cases were of patients who had been receiving spiritual healing.

I have told the story of the boy suffering from leukaemia who was expected to die, but who made a very remarkable recovery, his blood content being normal in a short time. He had been dosed with cortisone.

When the boy was at his weakest state and death was expected, we were asked to intercede for him. Within twenty-four hours a change for the better was noted, he had new strength and vitality and his blood content became normal.

So unusual and unexpected was the recovery that the boy was presented as a demonstration case before a panel of hospital doctors to show the evidence of the curative qualities of cortisone for leukaemia.

I heard about this, and had time to write to the professor in charge of the case, pointing out the boy's recovery was dated from the commencement of spiritual healing. The professor replied to me, ignoring the spiritual healing factor and stated the boy's recovery was due to cortisone.

SPIRITUAL HEALING CAN MISLEAD DOCTORS

A "blue baby" only a few weeks old, was dying in a London hospital. The doctors had tried to give the baby blood infusions but owing to the weakness of the baby they were not able to effect an insertion of the tube into the circulatory system.

The baby was expected to die within hours—certainly before morning. The parents were present at the time and were told of the position. They telephoned to me for absent healing telling me of the doctors' grim verdict. Absent healing was sought for the child immediately.

The baby did not die, and by morning he was stronger and the "blueness" was less. The baby continued to make progress. The doctors, observing this, decided to inject a serum, which the parents were informed was a new drug from America.

The baby fully recovered. Here was another case of a baby living and overcoming its disease, in defiance of all medical anticipation. So impressed were the doctors, they wrote a paper about it, emphasising the effectiveness of the new drug, and this paper was circulated to other hospitals and medical authorities, with the object of encouraging other doctors to use this drug. They were unaware of the intervention of spiritual healing, and even had they known of this, it is questionable whether they would have given it any credence. It can be reasonably assumed that the doctors were misled, and so advocated a new form of treatment based upon an incorrect assumption.

Over the years we have had evidence of similar occurrences. I recall another case of a woman who was pregnant and found to be suffering from nephritis. Her condition was said to be desperate and her life was in jeopardy. Surgery was deemed to be inadvisable. The value of many of the testimonies I cite in this book is observed when the change for the better has taken place within a few hours after spiritual healing has commenced for the patient. It was so with this woman.

Hitherto, so I was told, she had not been receiving any special medical treatment—it was thought her condition was too serious for this. As soon as it became apparent that the symptoms were decreasing, she was subjected to mild deep-ray therapy, a calculated risk in view of the pregnancy. In spite of the treatment, the woman continued to get well and all signs of her trouble disappeared. A normal baby was eventually born and the husband

and relatives were told how pleased the doctors were at the way the disease had surrendered to the deep-ray. Once again it is suggested that the doctors were misled, and doubtless were encouraged to treat other cases of nephritis in the same way.

It is natural that the doctors would wish to find out why a patient suffering from an "incurable" condition and expected to die, makes a remarkable recovery instead, so they cannot be blamed for attaching undue importance to the particular form of treatment then being employed.

In the course of our experience in healing, it is surprising how many times we have been told that patients, very seriously ill, are being given "a new and very expensive drug being flown in from America". It has happened scores of times. Sometimes I wonder whether this is a story told to the patients and their relatives for purely psychological effects in an effort to boost the morale of the patient or to soothe the anxiety of the relatives.

CHAPTER TWENTY-TWO

SPIRITUAL HEALING IS ALL-EMBRACING

Mrs. Freda Inglefield of Leamington Spa sent me a narrative telling of the different ways in which the healing power has helped her son, daughter and herself over a period of time. Here it is:

" 'What a remarkable improvement! I would never have believed it possible!' When the eye specialist spoke those cheering words to my daughter, my heart lifted.

"This was the second time a medical specialist had given such a verdict on one of my children. The first time it concerned my son. He was born with a valvular disease, but as the years went by, with spiritual healing, a rare change had taken place in him. His heart muscles had grown strong enough for the heart to work normally.

"And now my daughter, who had very poor eyesight, following operations for cataract, was being told her eyes were getting stronger—that she now needed only fine lenses.

"Could two such outstanding health improvements in one family be coincidence? I don't think so.

"I feel convinced it was through the powers of spiritual healer Harry Edwards that my children were put on the road to health. For their recovery began only from the time I first wrote to him.

"Though he has never met my son and daughter, Mr. Edwards prayed for them constantly, concentrating his healing powers upon them. And the seeming miracle occurred.

"My story of help through absent healing began sixteen years ago. In those days I was a very worried mother, terribly apprehensive about the future of my two teenage children. My son's heart was so weak, the slightest physical exertion tired him. My daughter, despite her pebble-lensed glasses, was unable even to see the blackboard at school. Then some friends gave me Mr.

Edwards's address—and I jumped at the idea of his help, for, because of my spiritual beliefs, I already felt faith in his spiritual healing powers.

"When I wrote to Mr. Edwards, he replied immediately, wanting details of my children's illnesses; asking me to send in a weekly report of their progress.

" 'We at Burrows Lea, have started intercession for your son and daughter,' he told me. 'At any time when you have a chance, give your thoughts to our prayers on their behalf.'

"Trustingly, hopefully, I followed Mr. Edwards's instructions. Each week, I duly wrote to him giving news of my son and daughter.

"They were always good reports. Soon after the absent healing started, I was able to tell him that my daughter could now see well enough to thread a needle. That my son could do little jobs around the house, like fetching coal.

"As time went by, as my children both astounded the doctors with their recoveries, my faith in Mr. Harry Edwards's spiritual healing powers was my mainstay.

"Then in one letter, I was able to report to Mr. Edwards my greatest joy. My son was getting married. His heart condition was such that the doctor had pronounced him fit to lead a normal life.

"With both my children grown up and healthy, my contact with Mr. Edwards ended. But years later, once again I had to call upon him.

"The year was 1958. My daughter had recently married and my son was already the father of four children. His former heart trouble forgotten, he was successfully running his own business.

"Then one day, my husband and I were having tea when my son's neighbour called at our house.

"As I heard him talking to my husband in the hall, I sensed something terrible had happened. My husband came back into the room and took me in his arms.

" 'You'll have to be brave,' he said, 'it's about our son.'

" 'Is he in hospital?' As my husband shook his head, I realised the truth.

" 'His van crashed into a lorry this afternoon. He was killed instantly.'

"At that moment my thoughts were not of myself, but of my son's widow and children.

"It was not until later that night, when I had returned from comforting his wife, that the tragedy of my own loss began to prey on my mind.

"In the midst of my sorrow, I remembered Mr. Edwards. I started a letter. 'Right now I feel only dazed,' I wrote, 'but I am afraid I'll have a reaction and my nerves will crack. Please help me.'

"By return of post came Mr. Edwards's reply: in sympathetic words he told me he and his helpers at Burrows Lea would intercede for me.

"That night, as I lay in bed thinking of my son, praying silently that God would give solace to those of us that loved him, I knew some spiritual power I could not define would give me the strength I needed.

"Looking back now, I know my strength came from God and the prayers, the compassion, the healing gifts of Harry Edwards all played their part in steadying my nerves and gave me the will power to carry on and help my family.

"I have told of two crises in my life when Mr. Harry Edwards's absent healing sustained me.

"I now know that, whatever happens in my life, I can always depend that his prayers will be with me.

"I feel that Mr. Edwards with his helpers at Burrows Lea are understanding friends, ready to assist when needed . . . never failing to answer an appeal. It is partly due to them that, despite the tragic happenings in my life, I still have faith in God and the goodness of man."

CHAPTER TWENTY-THREE

WHY SOME HEALINGS ARE SAID TO FAIL

WHEN doctors have been asked to comment upon the evidence for spiritual healing successes, they are apt to reply, "That's all very well, but what about the failures?"

It is true that healers look upon their successes to establish proof of healing, and why not? When it is recalled that people do not seek the aid of a healer for minor conditions, which usually yield to medicine or the recuperative power of the body, but for diseases and afflictions which are of long standing, unyieldable to medical practice, or in the "incurable category", then healers are justified in basing the case for spiritual healing upon successes.

Doctors do not stress their failure when a patient does not respond to recognised treatment; nor do they condemn drugging because it may induce deleterious side effects.

Unfortunately, healers encounter tragic results which have followed medical practice. It was Mr. Burton who once said: "We live in a sea of doctors' mistakes."

I have never known anyone to be caused suffering through spiritual healing.

We recognise that a healing can only take place within the scope of the physical and spirit laws that govern us all. This is the only limitation that can be applied to spiritual healing. Just as there must be a reasoned process behind every successful healing, so there must likewise be a reasoned process to explain why a healing may not have taken place.

Remembering the severity of "incurable" and chronic conditions we are called upon to heal there is less than twenty per cent which do not appear to benefit.

In Chapter Fourteen, I have told of the case of Mr. B. who had

WHY SOME HEALINGS ARE SAID TO FAIL

a malignant cancer of the bladder, and who eventually died from a heart attack. The doctors said he had died from cancer, and implied that spiritual healing had failed.

I recall the case of a little girl of five and a half, whom I will call Patricia. The following is her abbreviated medical history:

Patricia was admitted to the Park Royal Hospital suffering from leukaemia. The mother was told that this was incurable, and the doctors expected her to die within six months.

The mother reported:

"Patricia received blood transfusions, but gradually she was being reduced to a wax doll in appearance. We were told there was no hope whatever of her recovery, and we were reconciled for the worst. We even wished that God would take her rather than see her pine away, day by day.

"Drugs were flown from America for her—one drug was supposed to increase her appetite and bring colour to her cheeks. They did improve her appetite but failed to produce colour. They gave her the appearance of a bloated child. As the doctors considered the drugs were ineffective they were discontinued.

"We read of Mr. Harry Edwards's service at the Royal Albert Hall and through the *Daily Sketch* we got in touch with him. We had an interview with Mr. Edwards, and from this date a change took place with Patricia. It seemed she again came back to life. A lively spirit was noticeable in her and the doctors were very pleased.

"Patricia was allowed to come home for a short spell, though the specialist said she was by no means well enough to be allowed with us, for he thought it essential to have a day and night watch over her. He said she would die within a month.

"From this time onwards we have maintained close contact with Mr. Edwards, who has continued to give Patricia absent healing treatment.

'While she was in hospital, the disease went from limb to limb and finally settled in her legs which became lifeless. Now she can run and dance and perform acrobatic movements. Her colour is making an appearance very much, and from every angle the child seems perfectly cured. Her blood count is normal."

Patricia did not die and continued well for a further year, when a slight relapse took place. She was readmitted into the same hospital, where once again, with spiritual healing the blood content was quickly balanced.

Her health was restored and the hospital arranged for Patricia to be sent to a convalescent home to build up her general health. On the eve of her departure, Patricia fell out of bed and broke her shoulder bones and from the shock and ill-effects of this unhappy accident, she passed away. It should be noted that at this time her blood content was normal. The doctors declared she had died from leukaemia. It was said that spiritual healing had failed.

If the child had not fallen and broken her shoulder bones, she would not have died. I expressed the point of view to the doctors that they would not have said the child would suddenly die within three days if she had not fallen out of bed. I pointed out to the medical men that Patricia had made a recovery from the attack of leukaemia. Her blood count was reported to be normal when the accident took place and she was only being kept in hospital waiting for a bed in a convalescent home.

The doctors were adamant. They knew that we had been treating the child by absent healing and that she had lived a further year after they declared she must die, but they continued to maintain that she had died from leukaemia, and gave this as a reason for a spiritual healing failure.

Much depends, too, on the conduct of the patient after receiving healing treatment. There was the case of the man who came to the Sanctuary, crippled with pain from a slipped disc. He could not walk or move without agony. We removed the trouble, he was able to bend right over to touch his toes, and lean far back; he could walk freely, and had no pain at all. He went home a glad man. He felt so good, that he went out into his garden, took up a long handled axe and proceeded to split up the roots of a tree. It was not very long before he wrenched his back causing it to revert to its previous painful state. His conduct was unreasonable, for it gave the healing no chance to consolidate the betterment of his back. From this it may well have been said that the healing had failed. Fortunately, the man returned, very sorry for what he had done, so again we corrected the spinal alignment for him and with wiser conduct in the future his healing remained permanent.

WHY SOME HEALINGS ARE SAID TO FAIL

Disease and sickness arise from the law of cause and effect. So long as the causes are maintained then the effects will return.

The responsibility of the healing purpose is first to overcome the cause, and then remove the ill-effects. When the cause is a physical one, such as, for example, when the mechanism of an eye has been destroyed by surgery or an accident, it can be outside the province of healing to overcome the trouble.

Sometimes the cause can be collective—physical, mental and spirit; these three interact, one upon the other, but as the healing overcomes one of the causes, then usually the others are also seen to yield.

The healing influences deal directly with the spirit disharmony, and also direct soothing influencing to the consciousness to ease nervous tensions, fears, etc. By this means, the entire bodily health tone is improved, assisting the healing purpose to master the symptoms of stress. If the cause is purely physical, then a physical change must be sought for through the patient's habits and way of life.

We are often asked to help fading eyesight. There may be no actual disease but the eyes become tired and tense, and vision impaired. This is often accompanied by headaches and irritability, and the optician has to prescribe lenses of increasing strength. A few questions to the patient will ascertain that he or she is in the sort of employment that demands very close eye concentration. It may be a woman who is engaged on very fine needlework, or a draughtsman or tracer, whose work entails meticulous concentration on minute detail. Such patients may be in employment where the lighting conditions are not good, so being the direct cause of the weakening sight, and as long as they continue to work under such conditions so the cause is maintained and the eyesight will continue to suffer.

I recall the case of a woman who sought healing for her sight which was becoming misty. Her eyes were losing their focusing power, becoming hot and tense, and she needed powerful lenses to enable her to read. She had violent neuralgic pains and had to leave her book-keeping employment. We sought for healing to soothe the eyes and ease the nervous tensions, and we told her to "nurse" her eyes and avoid straining them. I remember pointing out to her that if she strained her arm she would rest it and possibly use a sling—so if she continued to use her eyes, straining them all the time to carry on her full daily functions, which included reading and television, then she was maintaining the cause of her difficulties. She followed this advice, and it was only a matter of a week or two before she found that the side effects of neuralgia and tenseness of the eyes went away. Her healing continued for some time, the vision becoming so clear that only low-powered lenses were necessary.

We were very pleased with this result, and so was the woman, too. She was so much better that we discontinued our intercessions on her behalf. Some time later, she returned to the Sanctuary with all the former ill-conditions. It transpired that she had become so much better that she felt she could resume her employment, and this she did. The result was that the *cause* was resurrected and so again the ill-effects followed.

This case is typical of many others, and it is surprising how many sufferers from strained eyesight refuse to even consider changing their manner of employment, which seems to them to be more important than their sight. They are prepared to accept blindness rather than seek a change. When we have reasoned with some patients, pointing out that their knowledge of their trade or profession was such that they could continue to give good service in some way that was not so exacting on their eyes, and induced them to discuss the matter with the management of the firm employing them, it has been invariably found that the management has been sympathetic and has arranged for another form of employment.

There was a young boy who was said to have been born with the skin eruption from which he suffered. His limbs were covered with hard angry-looking incrustations. They created pain and severe irritation and the boy was constantly crying with trouble. Life was a misery to him. His parents told me they had rarely enjoyed a full night's sleep without being disturbed by their son.

I saw this boy once in his home in a nearby village, and it was clear to see that he was very temperamental, restless, unhappy and depleted in health. We continued to treat this boy by absent healing to tranquilise the nerve tensions, and give relief. I was able to induce the parents to arrange for the lad to go and stay with some

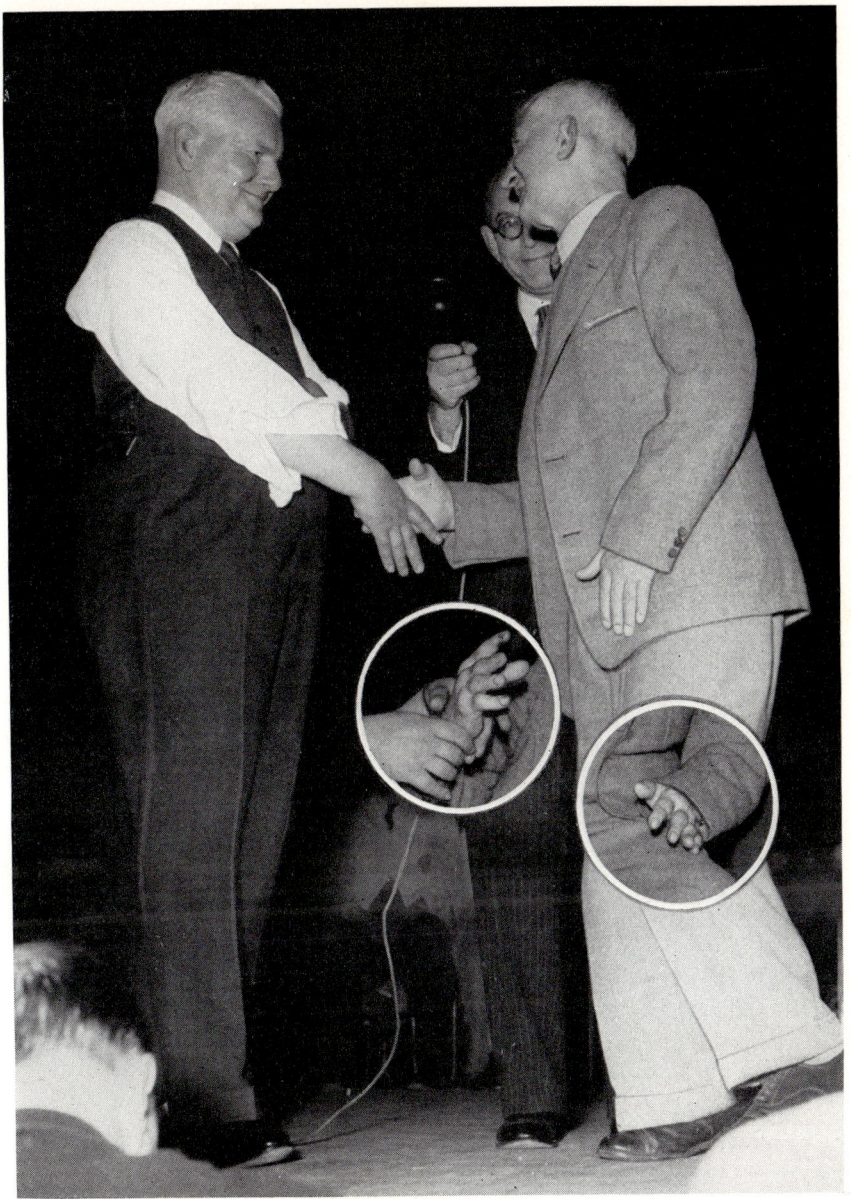

Another healing of an arthritic sufferer: note the hands before and after treatment

Checking the morning's post of absent healing letters

relatives for a while, which gave the parents some much-needed relief and helped them, too. The boy stayed away for about three months and during this time, his skin almost cleared. All anger left the skin and the areas affected decreased in size and all but disappeared. When he returned home, the only signs remaining were some red patches behind his knee. His attitude had become tractable, he was obedient, enjoyed his playing, and his conscience was happy and tranquil.

Then came some bad news. After the boy had been home for a while, the skin trouble began to return. I was again consulted, and in my conversation with the mother I found out that the boy was afraid of the dark, and the father—a good and kindly man—thought it best for his son to have to fight his fear to "make a man of him" and so made him go upstairs, round the dark corner by himself, and refused to allow him even a small night light in his room or on the landing. The purpose, of course, was to make the boy conquer his fears. The result was, as the mother told me, her boy dreaded the time when he had to go upstairs to bed, and even when she had put him into bed and tucked him in before putting out the light, she would feel her son trembling all over.

It seemed clear to me that this was the cause recreating fear in the boy's mind, inducing within severe neurosis, sadly affecting his health and reviving the skin disease. I told the mother my opinion and suggested she spoke to her husband, to allow, as an experiment, a small light to be put on the dark corner of the landing, and leaving the bedroom door open so that should the boy wake up in the night, he would be reassured. The father agreed and this was done. Two good results followed: the boy lost his fear of going upstairs and would do so unaccompanied, and after a reasonably short time his skin progressively cleared once again.

This healing succeeded because we were able to eliminate the *cause* which created a sense of fearfulness and terror in the boy's mind. If this had not taken place, and the father's attitude persisted, the boy's fears would have become intensified and there is no knowing what other ill-effects would have developed . . . and the healing effort declared a failure.

A final illustration in this connection concerns an elderly man and his wife, both victims of rheumatoid arthritis. Their hands were knarled and knotted, the finger joints enlarged and very painful, with little movement. All the other joints were sadly affected, movement was limited, and both of them had to use sticks to help them shuffle along. It was sad to think of this couple approaching their ending years, suffering pain and so severely handicapped.

They came for personal healing at the Sanctuary and we were able to bring about a measurable degree of easement. Their arms could stretch upwards, the wrists became mobile, and the fingers more flexible. They could walk much easier than they had done for years.

They came again some time later, when I saw that all the improvements had vanished and they were just as crippled as they were before. There had to be a reason for it, and my first question to them provided the answer—I asked them if their home was damp.

"Yes, it is," they said, "*very* damp, the walls are wet and even our shoes get mildewed overnight." They were living in an old village cottage, and there was no alternative accommodation. Here was a very clear example of the cause of the arthritis being maintained and no one could expect the healing to do very much while they were compelled to live under such uncongenial and unhygienic conditions.

There is another class of affliction in which spiritual healing is sometimes said to be ineffective, as in the following case. One afternoon a car drew up at the Sanctuary door and a young woman was carried inside. I was sent for, and it quickly became obvious that the patient, whose legs dangled quite lifelessly, was suffering rom total paralysis from the waist down—the effects from poliomyelitis. No matter how hopeless any condition may appear, we never fail to make an effort to see what good can be done, so I sat down in front of her and was about to make "contact", when she asked me: "Can I telephone from here?" I said: "Yes, of course you can." She almost took our breath away as she added: "My mother is waiting by the telephone to hear me tell her 'I can walk!'."

It was as sad as it was tragic. Some over-enthusiastic person had told her mother, "You only have to get your daughter down to Harry Edwards and for him to put his hands on her, for her to

WHY SOME HEALINGS ARE SAID TO FAIL

walk again." The mother and daughter were convinced, and so, without even waiting to make an appointment in the ordinary way, they hired a car and the girl and a friend arrived unexpected, anticipating an immediate and miraculous healing.

This kind of procedure is by no means isolated. Often patients with their dear ones will arrive at the Sanctuary at all hours, just out of the blue, often having travelled long distances on the off-chance of finding me at home. Some are lucky, but there are also those times when I and my associates are away conducting a public healing service somewhere in the United Kingdom and such patients find they have undertaken a fruitless journey.

We felt very sorry for the young girl, and, contrary to our custom, it was arranged that she would stay with us for a while, if only to give her the satisfaction of knowing that we did try to do everything we could for her with daily treatment, before she went back home. Actually we did succeed in getting some signs of returning co-ordination, but not very much.

So it is that when a disease (such as in the case quoted above) has developed so strongly that the nerves have come completely useless, having lost the power of function and possibly disintegrated altogether, healing is powerless to restore them. It is contrary to the law. Similar situations arise when, through surgery, certain nerves have had to be severed, or the function of an eye destroyed; or, where spinal meningitis with children has destroyed the function of hearing, so we are compelled to accept the situation that spiritual healing cannot restore that which does not exist. If I had one of my fingers amputated, then I should not expect—or ask for—a new one to grow.

This introduces an ethical argument, so often put forward by leaders of religion, who declare "If you had enough faith, to God all things are possible." If nothing takes place, then the priest has the escape route open, that the patient had "not enough faith". I suppose it would not be unfair to say to the priest "If you had enough faith, then I should be healed." All healings must take place within the scope of the laws that control us, and it is futile, to expect God to over-ride His laws of creation, in an act of favourable dispensation, for an individual.

True, we see healings take place, when doctors have declared a person to be incurable; but when these occur, they take place *within the laws*, and it means that medical science has not reached that state of wisdom enjoyed by the spirit doctors.

When we are faced with a situation, in which, under the scheme of things a recovery is not possible, we must not overlook the help that is given to the sufferer in granting easement from pain, inner peace and fortitude, and the necessary strength to enable the patient to be free from stress during the critical days and hours before the passing occurs.

We have observed this many times, particularly with people dying from malignant cancer. Spiritual healing is invoked at the eleventh hour. The infiltration of the cancerous cells has entered into the whole bodily system, and the patient is in great distress and under heavy sedation. It is in situations like this that the healing is able to give that peace to the body and mind enabling the passing to be a tranquil one. The healing has not been able to save the patient's life, and the case may come into the category of "failure". But can it *really* be said that an act of healing has not taken place, when contrary to the expectation of a turbulent passing, the sufferer is gently taken into spirit life?

There was a postman nearing the age of retirement, who would proudly tell you that he had never been ill in his life. Then one day he experienced acute internal pain. He was sent to an Epsom hospital, where he was operated upon and found to possess an inoperable cancer. He was sewn up and sent home to die—and this was expected to be imminent. We were asked to seek healing for him, and we visited him in his home and laid hands upon him. After a while all pain left him, his appetite returned and he recovered vitality, and I recall my visits to him, when he would delight in playing a miniature kind of zither when he and his family would join together in singing hymns.

His local doctor had been informed by the hospital of the diagnosis, and received instruction to give him daily morphia injections. Weeks went by, and the man did not die. All symptoms of the cancer disappeared, but the doctor ignored this, and continued to give the injections. The son spoke to the doctor and asked him not to give the injections for a while to see how his father would respond without them.

The doctor was told how spiritual healing had benefited the patient, that he was in no pain, and there were no symptoms of

WHY SOME HEALINGS ARE SAID TO FAIL

trouble, but he brushed the explanations aside with the rather brutal comment: "It's better for your father to die of morphine poisoning than cancer." The man continued to live, without any stress, for nearly a year, gradually getting weaker as the injections were persisted in, and so it was that eventually he *did* die from morphine poisoning and medical ignorance through incredulity. Thus another spiritual healing was said to have "failed".

Then there are those people who, strange as it may seem, ask for healing but who do not wish to be healed. The application for healing is just something else to add to the regiment of jars, bottles and lines of medicants they display. I recently met a lady who could not find her purse in her bulky bag, for all the bottles, etc., of medicines in it. There was the man who wrote: "Please do not make me too well, because I do not want to lose my disablement pension."

I remember a sharp-eyed little old lady who was brought to see me by her relatives. She was in a wheel-chair. I was told that she could not use her legs. True, she had arthritis, but when I sought for freedom of movement within the joints I found it not bad at all. I could not understand why she could not lift her arms upwards over her head, so I took it that I was mistaken. When I came to seek easement for her legs I found the evidence of arthritis, but only in a mild form. I was nonplussed. The alert old lady saw my puzzlement and knew that I did not think she was so bad at all, and I sensed she was afraid I should say something in the presence of her daughter who was with her.

She beckoned me close to her, and whispered words to the effect that she had worked for her family all her life, and they expected her to go on slaving for them, so she was taking advantage of her arthritis to have a rest! I observed the twinkle in her eye and sensed her sense of humour, as she hoped I would become a conspirator with her. I whispered back: "When you are alone, you can walk about O.K." and she nodded.

Perhaps it was that this old lady's sense of humour appealed to my own, so I did not give her away. I asked the daughter to give her mother all the nourishment and things she liked to have, to deal gently with her, and I felt no regret; the mother and I exchanged a message of understanding with our eyes, as she was wheeled away.

It is not possible to generalise when a healing does not take place. Each case is individual, but the overall reason is that when a condition has become too advanced, the body becoming too weakened, wasted or senile, then it is outside the scope of the physical and spiritual laws for the cause and ill-effects to be taken away.

CHAPTER TWENTY-FOUR

THIRTY YEARS

THE period covered in this book is thirty years.

In the years commencing with this century, spiritual healing was an haphazard affair. From time to time there were gifted healers, working in isolation, and the impact they made upon the national outlook was meagre and spasmodic.

Thirty years ago, spiritual healing was suspect, and it seemed to be desirable to prove to the medical profession and the Church that spiritual healing was a reality.

We did not get very far. We had then, as we have today, difficulty in obtaining official medical histories, X-ray photographs, etc., and needed to rely upon the information given to us by the patients and their relatives or friends. Nevertheless, in a number of cases we were able to obtain sufficient data to establish beyond all reasonable doubt outstanding healings of "incurability". When we passed on the healing story, supported by the names of hospitals, doctors and reported diagnoses and prognoses (which doctors were apt to deny), our claims for the healings to be recognised were invariably met with evasions, sometimes of the most fantastic kind.

My most bitter disillusionment came with the Archbishops' Commission on Divine Healing. When its formation was announced I thought at long last the time had arrived and that it was our opportunity to obtain recognition of spiritual healing as a proven healing agency. My hopes rose when the Commission asked me to supply evidential cases of spiritual healing.

I reported over seventy cases of supernormal healings, relating to incurable diseases, which had taken place during the previous three months. I thought such recent cases must still be fresh in the minds of the doctors and medical histories could be obtained easily.

When I attended the Commission I saw all this evidence swept aside, with indifference under the excuse that they could all be "spontaneous" healings and therefore were not spiritual healings. I was again asked to supply a few cases, with complete records, of supernormal healings, and I offered to the Commission the eight cases I have mentioned in Chapter Fourteen.

Although there were a number of medical people on the Commission, it did not feel competent to form a judgement, so the British Medical Association was asked to give an independent report and thus the British Medical Association appointed a special committee of doctors to study, investigate and report to the Commission its findings on the eight cases.

I requested, over and over again, for the right to see the committee's findings, so that I could, if necessary, comment upon them; but this was denied to me.

This committee issued its report, which I have quoted from in Chapter Fourteen. The investigation proved to be no investigation at all. *It did not ask for even one medical history relating to the cases. It did not ask for the attendance of even one of the patients to confirm the diagnosis or to verify the patient's recovery as claimed.*

Then came the shattering conclusion published in the Commission's Report that it had ruled it was "outside its terms of reference" to study the evidence for spiritual healing.

It became very clear that both the Church and medicine were determined to ignore, at all costs, the evidence of healings attained through spiritual healers.

This forced me to the conclusion that we could not expect any justice or fair play from either body, and it was a waste of time to deal further with them.

I made it known at that time that we would welcome a bona fide investigation of spiritual healing, as we do today, but that we should not co-operate if the medical profession was to be the judge and jury giving no right of appeal.

Any investigation should be conducted by a panel of people, experienced in the art of assessing the value of evidence at which both the medical profession and ourselves would have the right of cross-examination. For example: if we provide evidence for a healing of an abdominal cancer and the medical answer to this is "There was a wrong diagnosis", then the panel would be able to study the whole medical history, to question the doctors who made the original diagnosis and if there had been pathological tests, the laboratory evidence should be available.

I do not expect the medical profession ever to assent to such terms. It would undermine their sacrosanct position of being the Final Authority, whose word must not be questioned.

Let me give two examples of this type of medical autocracy.

Before the Archbishops' Commission was formed, there was a previous private investigation into spiritual healing undertaken by a doctor with high qualifications. I supplied to him one hundred cases of supernormal healings which had followed spiritual healing treatment.

Case 1. A man was pathologically proved by biopsy to be suffering from a malignant cancerous condition of the throat. He had all the usual symptoms—severe pain and swelling, he could not swallow, and his voice deteriorated into a hoarse whisper. He was to be operated upon in two weeks' time.

When the man knew of this verdict he telephoned me for absent healing. In the immediate days following, the pains left him and the swellings subsided; and his voice returned to normal. Two days before the operation was due to take place he requested a further examination by the two specialists who had conducted the previous examinations. After exhaustive tests and a fresh biopsy, they declared that all symptoms of the cancer had disappeared.

The two specialists were then informed that spiritual healing had been given to this man, and his recovery attributed to that. What, then was the opinion of the two specialists and had they any alternative explanation?

This was the unbelievable—almost laughable—explanation they gave in all seriousness: "That by a fortunate coincidence the section of tissue taken for the biopsy, happened to contain all carcinomatous tissue."

Case 2. This refers to a registered blind woman. When her blindness commenced she was under the care of Moorfields Eye Hospital. She became totally blind, and could not distinguish light from darkness for many years. She was brought to the Sanctuary and while receiving treatment from Mrs. Olive Burton, she exclaimed, "I can see!" Her degree of vision was slight at first but she could distinguish the shape of objects, and she recognised a flower held before her. In the days that followed her vision strengthened so much so that she could see tolerably well. She went back to hospital to see if they could help her with glasses to be told that these could not be supplied to the "registered blind".

When the doctors were asked to comment on her recovery the reply was: "The woman had only to be told she could see and she did." I should have liked to have had the opportunity to ask the doctors why they had themselves not suggested "she could see".

In case readers may think I am exaggerating, they will find these medical "explanations" given in the *British Medical Journal* of December 4th, 1954, without comment as supplying sufficient answer to account for these healings.

Can it be wondered at, that after these experiences and the treatment given to spiritual healing by the Archbishops' Commission that we no longer concern ourselves with trying to obtain acknowledgement of spiritual healing with either the Church or the medical profession?

We have no need to prove spiritual healing today, for it has become an accepted part of our national life. It is accepted by the national Press who no longer regard our healings as "news". It has been proven in countless thousands of homes where health and happiness has been restored, through the healing of the sick.

Further evidence of national support was found after I had made a B.B.C. television appearance. The B.B.C. received a greater mass of correspondence after this programme than with any other at that time, and this induced them to conduct a national survey, when it was found that over *ninety per cent* of those interrogated reported they believed in spiritual healing and of this number over sixty per cent believed in the kind of spiritual healing that healers practice.

When some two hundred and fifty hospital authorities granted permission for healer members of the National Federation of Spiritual Healers to visit and, with medical sanction, minister to patients in over one thousand five hundred of our National Hospitals, the British Medical Association became annoyed. They passed a resolution at an annual conference deploring this and urging the hospital authorities to withdraw their permission. It organised questions in Parliament to obtain the Minister of Health's ruling that healers should not be allowed entry into the National Service Hospitals, but the Minister would not give this. The Church joined in the campaign and at least one bishop wrote a letter to *The Times* in protest. The British Medical Association wrote to all the Hospital Authorities, requesting them to withdraw the permission they had given for healers to treat the sick in the hospitals under their jurisdiction and out of the two hundred and fifty authorities who had given permission only nineteen obeyed the order.

Such permission still stands today, and it is interesting to note that not one complaint has been received concerning the conduct of Federation Healers when attending patients in hospital.

More and more doctors are showing their sympathy and co-operation with spiritual healing by frequently sending their patients and their relatives for healing treatment, and let it also be said, come *themselves* for treatment, too.

We need to observe secrecy when doctors do this, for if it became known that they were "associating" with healers who are not registered practitioners, they would be liable to disciplinary action by the British Medical Council. Happily this has never happened. We also find that hospitals more freely allow in-patients to be brought to the Sanctuary, sometimes in ambulances with nurses in attendance.

The same story is being observed with clergymen of all denominations, who write for absent healing for their parishioners who are sick and then accompany them to the Sanctuary. We have even known Roman Catholic priests request healing for themselves.

So it will be appreciated that today, we have no need to prove healing to the medical profession and the clergy.

The phenomenal growth of spiritual healing during these past thirty years has arisen from success in the healing of the sick from all manner of diseases, when doctors could do no more for them. The high ratio of recoveries that take place with less chronic complaints has also contributed to the advance that healing has earned. If there had not been this success then the healing movement would have waned and frittered away years ago.

The greater part of our healing ministry at the Sanctuary in Shere is conducted by absent (or distant) healing. The post, including letters from all over the world, average ten thousand letters a week and in 1966 we received our ten millionth letter.

Each year about five thousand people come to the Sanctuary to receive or observe spiritual healing. This is only a small percentage of all those who ask for healing appointments, and it is *time* which prevents more patients being received.

The National Federation of Spiritual Healers in 1965 became ten years of age. Its total membership has grown from a few hundreds in 1955 to nearly five thousand. The growth of spiritual healing is world-wide, and the Federation in 1965 affiliated Associations in Canada, Australia, New Zealand and South and South-West Africa, thus leading the way towards an International Federation. In addition to the above, there are other healing guilds, and there are many other healers who heal privately not desiring to join any group or organisation.

That is the picture of spiritual healing today.

It is all the more remarkable when it is known that, with a few exceptions, healers carry out their merciful work in their spare time after the daily round of employment has been completed. Healers are inspired to do their work by the feelings of love and compassion for the sick. These are spiritual qualities.

Once, in an interview I gave to a doctor who was the medical correspondent of a national newspaper, I asked him if he could account for recoveries taking place through healing that were contrary to medical expectation. He said two things that impressed me.

The first was, that people go to doctors to get treatment whereas they go to a healer to get well.

The second observation was, that healers give their personal time, love and attention to a patient who is said to be incurable, whereas a doctor, who is dealing with sickness as a professional duty, is unable to give his love and the time necessary to assist every patient as he may like to do.

Healers universally agree that healing is God's gift to all His people irrespective of race or creed. They recognise that their gift of healing is a contribution towards the fulfilment of the Divine Plan for the spiritual progression of all souls.

In the past spiritual healing has been a mysterious thing, and probably through our lack of understanding we have tended to make it so. The word "miracle" has become commonly associated with healing, and it is interesting to note that this word has been used more by doctors and surgeons than anyone else in describing recoveries that they cannot understand.

In studying the pattern of the healing of specific diseases we are advancing in an appreciation of the healing processes themselves, and the advance of science in the study of "energies" has provided us with the answers to many questions that hitherto were unknown. To the human mind a miracle is only a miracle as long as we do not know the means by which it is performed.

At our Sanctuary the volume of absent healing is so great (ten thousand letters a week) that it is a physical impossibility under present circumstances to keep individual case records, but when letters come telling of an outstanding recovery, these letters are kept and the pertinent extracts taken from them to give the essence of the healing story.

In my book *The Evidence for Spirit Healing* are over 6,000 such citations, related in the course of four years' healing. Every year since then we have collected such reports, which on average exceed several per day, for every day of the year.

To give an idea of this, a few typical extracts follow on; these have been selected to give an idea of the diversity of healings which take place, and all are taken from the recorded healings in the first month of 1965 when the manuscript of this book was in preparation. All these are cases where absent healing only has been employed:

"I have wonderful news about Mr. X. It seemed impossible that anything could happen to change him, but his wife told me he is a changed man . . . he has given up gambling and is altogether different."

"Mrs. X was in the operating theatre when the postman brought your letter. I rang her husband . . . and he told me the doctor had rung him up from the hospital and said the surgeon did not find what they had expected but only evidence that healing had taken place. They did not remove anything and stitched her up."

"I sought your aid for Mr. X who was in the advanced stage of cancer and a miracle was performed. He is back at work. I saw him for the first time since his illness three years ago. He was dancing and his old cheery self."

"It is now twelve months since I first wrote to you and my doctor's last words were that he could do nothing more for me and that the swelling would not go down. I have not seen or heard from my doctor since. People who saw me a year ago are so astonished at seeing me a normal woman."

"My husband is a changed personality. He is kind, even-tempered and generous. For the first time in twenty-five years of married life, we have enjoyed a real Christmas together. My heart is full of joy."

"Her family waited for her death. That night . . . she slept . . . In the morning she told the doctor she had had immense sweating which had a very bad smell. She added, 'During the night I regained my health, I am quite well and I am hungry.' The doctor could not understand what had happened to her."

"I asked for your co-operation in removing a lump from my wife's groin, which has completely disappeared."

"We had some wonderful news. Our son paid his three-monthly visit to the specialist and he told us that our son's eyes had improved and were very much clearer."

"My eyesight is practically cured . . . I need not go to see the doctor for nine months . . . he was so pleased. Double cataract and glaucoma at seventy-six. I should say it is a miracle."

"Three years ago I asked you for healing for my friend's mother. She was suffering from cancer . . . she is quite well now."

"Re Doctor X. Since you got my telegram the condition is so much better . . . the doctors speak of a wonder . . . eating again without vomiting and is able to laugh, and sleep without drugs."

"When I wrote to you I had a very crooked back. That night I was able to lie down and my back touched the bed completely. My bad leg and hip did not hurt me . . . I looked in the mirror and my back was straight, my shoulders were back and I was two inches taller."

"You will be pleased to hear that old Mr. X, bedfast for a year, has given his wife a big surprise. He got up and dressed, is free from choking . . . and sleeps."

"My son had a cystocsopy and an arteriogram performed on

him. To the utter astonishment and confusion of the two specialists, the horrible protuberance shown on the X-rays has completely disappeared. X is now perfectly fit."

"My friend is now able to get up and walk. The doctors say they cannot understand it, as they never expected her to walk again."

"She was waiting for an operation for a malignant tumour when my father wrote to you. When she was admitted to hospital, the specialists and staff were astounded that they could no longer find any trace of the growth."

And so they go on. Last year there were five hundred similar stories.

It must be true to say that each of these and all other healings are planned acts. There is such a wide diversity of diseases healed, that each case must be individual and needs a planned treatment. There must be an intelligence capable of truly diagnosing the cause of the sickness and possessing the knowledge how to apply the corrective forces necessary to bring about the healing. These healing intelligences must possess a superior knowledge to man, for "incurability" denotes that human intelligence has come to a halt.

For the reason that there must exist a state of harmony between that which is transmitted and that which is received, it indicates a state of attunement between the source of the healing and the patient—that of Spirit. If the healing intelligence is not human then it must be of Spirit. Thus spiritual healing demonstrates a kinship between the people on earth and those in Spirit.

Let me conclude by giving a transcript of the address I gave at the Service of Reunion and Remembrance at the Royal Albert Hall on Armistice Sunday, November 14th, 1965:

"I would like to give you three illustrations.

"Robert Schumann, the famous composer died in 1856, over a century ago.

"Seventy-seven years later, in the home circle of the Swedish Minister in London, Schumann's Spirit communicated through a medium to the renowned violinist Miss D'Aranyi, and told her of a violin concerto he had composed, and bid her search for this.

"After seeking news of the concerto from all known sources, the Spirit of Schumann finally directed her to the Prussian State

Library in Berlin, where after an intensive search the lost concerto was found lying in a cellar amid a pile of unrecorded contributions. "This concerto was first publicly played on the B.B.C. radio on October 20th, 1937, with Miss D'Aranyi playing the solo part.

"The undeniable fact is, that no one knew of the existence of this music, and were it not for the spirit messages received from Schumann himself, the concerto would have been lost for all time."

(At this point I asked the pianist on the platform to play a short excerpt from this concerto.)

"*This is an illustration of spirit communication.*

"I am holding in my hand an amulet. It is made of Thebian glass, the quality of which determines its age as being 3,500 years old. The hieroglyphics engraved on it declare it to be the amulet belonging to the 'Custodian of the Southern Countries of Egypt'. It was a possession of a Pharaoh of those days.

"This amulet was given to me in the presence of others through mediumship. It was brought from its resting-place in Egypt in a fraction of time through the walls of the seance room and placed in my hands.

"*This is an illustration of spirit science.*

"About twelve years ago, a healer carried a boy of ten years of age on to the platform of a Healing Service in the Victoria Halls, London, organised by the Spiritualist Society of Great Britain.

"The boy had to be carried, because he was a total spastic. His knees were fast, the lower legs were bent backwards against the thighs and the legs drawn up, immovable, to his chest. His arms were similarly affected. A pitiful specimen of humanity—totally medically incurable.

"At that service his healing commenced—his joints received movement. With patient treatment week by week, his affliction was progressively overcome.

"Two years ago, he walked, with only a faint limp, down the aisle of a church with his bride on his arm.

"*This is an illustration of spiritual healing.*

"These are not isolated instances of Spirit power—they can be repeated a thousand-fold. Tonight you have witnessed through the mediumship of Nora Blackwood and Stanley Poulton communication between earthly and Spirit life. Tonight in thousands of churches, throughout the land, mediums are giving clairvoyance bringing comfort to the bereaved and guidance to those in need.

"At the same time, Spirit teachings are being delivered to show us the right way to live in God's sight.

"Every day, healers are restoring health and happiness to countless numbers of afflicted people, often when medical science can do no more for them.

"*This is Spiritualism in our time.*

"What is its ultimate purpose?

"It is the proving by demonstration, through the gifts of the Spirit, the truth that we are all akin to Spirit in this life now, and that there is a spiritual heritage before each one of us, when this earthly phase of life has ended.

"In this material and scientific age, spiritual values have declined; the orthodox churches are losing their power, because no longer are the people willing to accept religion as an act of blind faith with unquestioning obedience. Yet they are spiritually hungry. They are looking for spiritual leadership and guidance.

"Before they are willing to accept any positive idea, they rightly ask for its truth to be demonstrated as a truth, and so prove that it is so.

"This is precisely what Spiritualism does. It is the purpose of mediumship.

"What are the lessons we can learn from the healing by Spirit means of one who is said to be medically incurable. Every healing must be a planned act. To carry out a plan needs intelligence. Obviously when a so-called 'incurable' is healed through Spirit intervention, then a wiser intelligence than that of man comes into the picture. If that intelligence is not human, then it can only be from Spirit.

"Healers do not heal of themselves, they are but the channels through whom the healing forces flow to the patient. Therefore, they must be in a state of affinity with Spirit to be so used.

"It is a law that there must be a state of harmony between any form of transmission and reception, therefore the patient must be able to attune with Spirit, in order to receive from it.

"Thus healing demonstrates the truth that we are all part Spirit in our physical life.

"The same conclusions can be easily seen with other gifts of the

Spirit like clairvoyance. The medium is able to receive Spirit vision in order to bring our dear ones in Spirit back to us so evidentially, and to receive communication from them to prove their personalities. Thus the realms of life are linked together proving yet again there is no division between them.

"Is this proving of kinship with Spirit just academic, or has it a much deeper purpose? It has, as I will try to show.

"If only for a few moments, let us remember that this is the Remembrance Service held on Armistice Sunday and all that it means. Twenty-five years ago this night (less than a third of lifetime) death and destruction was falling from the skies on London and our other cities . . . and in return we were doing the same on people and cities in other lands. Today, we are not free from the threat of total destruction.

"We need to overcome the evil of racial discrimination. We live in times of great wealth and abject poverty. Materialism rules the world with its struggle for power and the rule of money.

"But all this cannot subjugate the spiritual qualities that are inherent in man. From the earliest times, spiritual progress has been recorded, accelerated with the evolution of high ideals and appreciation of spiritual values. We have a far higher concept of these than our forefathers did. Life is more sacred. Brutalities and cruelties are more abhorred. Slavery has become an iniquity. We no longer permit child labour in the mines. We take care of the aged and the infirm. When animals are ill-treated, public opinion is aroused in protest. We support good causes like Oxfam to feed and clothe the destitute.

"These are the signs of spiritual consciousness—but there is still more to be done:

"The purpose of Spiritualism today, through mediumship and healership is to awaken the conscience of the human family, to a consciousness of spiritual values through knowledge and understanding, so that through logic and the evidence we demonstrate, we show the way towards new incentives to overcome the materialistic and ignoble ways of selfish life today.

"In their place, will come the acceptance of spiritual kinship with Spirit and thereby with God, leading towards the coming of the true brotherhood of man, accepting common responsibilities towards each other.

"This then is the ultimate purpose which underlies our teaching based on the truth of kinship with Spirit and survival after earthly death.

"So it becomes our mission to spread this knowledge, and it is our common concern. This is a people's affair; we have no great organisation or wealth behind us. Indeed, we have to convert the vested interests of both Church and medicine—and this is a major task. What we do possess is, the most powerful weapon of all, that of the public conscience, where our truths are being treasured in the hearts and homes of the people.

"No truth can ever be suppressed for ever, it must emerge and triumph in the end. We do not depend upon great national leaders. It is *you*, the people, who are the leaders today, as you make known to your neighbours and friends the eternal truths which we prove by demonstration, so you will play your part in the furtherance of the Divine Plan.

'As you adopt a spiritual code of values in your lives, seeking to do no harm to anyone, rendering service to your fellows, fighting for those good causes which embrace peace, justice, brotherhood and an awareness of responsibility to our brethren—the animal kingdom—so shall we more quickly establish a right of way of living in God's sight, promoting the progression of all souls.

"This Divine plan is our heritage, and Spiritualism is its spearpoint. Let us through our endeavour, give a greater promise of right living for those who will follow on after us, adding a more lustrous chapter of the future, entitled 'The Spiritual Emanicipation of Mankind'."

POSTSCRIPT

THIS book was projected in the Spring of 1965. It is now Spring 1968. During these three past years much has happened. Spiritual healing has continued to make great strides forward everywhere.

At the Sanctuary, Burrows Lea, Shere, the requests for both personal and absent healing continue to grow, week by week. In 1966 we received our ten-millionth letter; our post sways around the ten thousand mark every week. We now have affiliated Associations in Canada; Australia; New Zealand, where a government charter has been given to the Association; South and South-West Africa: in addition, liaison officers and representatives have been appointed for the U.S.A., Continental and other countries.

In 1965 Mr. Gordon Turner and I produced a Study Course on Spiritual Healing which has been said to be the most important aid to healership yet devised. We also conducted the well-remembered Teach-In at the Central Hall, Westminster, London, S.W.1., presenting the Mid-Twentieth Century Approach to Healing.

In 1967 the Harry Edwards (N.F.S.H.) Trust was inaugurated for the purpose of assisting healers in times of adversity. This has received a splendid response with over £1,700 being subscribed in ten months. The N.F.S.H. Headquarters also arranged for a very successful Healing Service and Demonstration in the Free Trade Hall in Manchester.

All these activities, in addition to the normal administration work in connection with the Federation, imposed considerable strain upon the facilities available at Burrows Lea, so much so that about Easter time last year Olive Burton made the firm declaration that funds must be raised to enable the Federation to have its own central headquarters in London and to be adequately staffed. Thus it was, at the Federation's Annual Conference last July, she proposed that a special campaign be started to gather in sufficient funds to achieve this objective *within twelve months*. This meant raising at least £20,000, plus an annual maintenance reserve. To do this in twelve months seemed, at the time, a fantastic, if not impossible, task. Supported by a small committee, Olive Burton and I prepared three schemes which, at the time of writing, are already in being or in preparation. On paper and in our expectant hopes, with co-operation from all our members and friends, we can now begin to realise the expectancy of reaching our target. The first scheme brought in over £6,000 in four months after all expenses had been met.

Thus, in 1968, we find we have to attend two Summer Schools for Healers in Torquay and Blackpool; to produce two Federation Reviews, and maintain the monthly Magazine "The Spiritual Healer"; to help through a new Federation Constitution; to carry the fund-raising schemes to establish a new central headquarters combined with a healing centre; and above all to maintain even more strongly the Spiritual Healing work of the Sanctuary. In addition, Olive Burton and I have accepted an invitation to attend a country-wide Healers' Congress in South Africa, holding two large healing services with demonstrations in Durban and Cape Town, not to mention attending other functions, giving lectures and conducting healing services in large towns in the United Kingdom.

I remember making up my mind to retire when I reached the age of sixty-five in 1958, but could not do so. This May I shall be seventy-five and am now reconciled and content to carry on the healing mission until the time arrives to rest finally from this willing and rewarding labour.

In 1967, "The Harry Edwards Spiritual Healing Sanctuary, Shere, Surrey," received charitable status from the Charity Commissioners, and arrangements are being made, in which we hope to ensure, that the Sanctuary will be preserved as a centre for spiritual healing for all time.

So the thirty years of healership is now thirty-three, and all being well, I look for the opportunity of carrying on this mission for some time to come.

INDEX

INDEX

abscess, 17
absent healing, 27, 38, 40, 47, 50, 66–67, 86
Addison's disease, 64
animal healer, 62
Archbishop's Commission on Divine Healing, 98, 106, 119, 147, 150
arthritis, 36–39, 41, 45, 72, 121, 122, 141, 145
Asian 'flu epidemic, 66
astral travelling, 24

Baden-Powell, Lady, 94
Balham Spiritualist Church, 23
Bangor healing demonstration, 1964, 31
Barker, Sir Herbert, 45
Beck Dr., 108,
Blackwood, Nora, 156
"blue baby", 131
Bonham Carter, Mr., 99
brain disease, 47
British Medical Association, 46, 130, 148, 150
British Medical Council, 45, 150
British Medical Journal, 45, 60
Burton, Mrs. Olive, 36, 52, 53, 55, 75, 97, 98
Burton, Edwina, 97
Burton, George, 43, 91, 98, 115, 136

cataract, 133

cause and effect, 139–40
childbirth, 110–11
clairvoyance, 158
clubfoot, 28
collapsed lung, 28
Cudd, Mrs. Gladys, 26–30
Cyprus healing mission, 52

Daily Sketch, 137
D'Aranyi, Miss, 155–6
deep-ray therapy, 131
Doble, Mr., 122
drug addiction, 50
Duke of Athlone, 40

eyesight, 83, 139, 150, 154
Evidence for Spirit Healing, The, 153

Ferdinando, Mrs., 123–6
first contact healing, 27
first "surgical" healing, 6

gastric ulcer, 74, 108
Goodliffe, Philip, 57–59
Governor of Guernsey, 41–42
Great Ormond St. Hospital, 99
growths, 64, 102
Gunckel, Mr. and Mrs., 51

"hakim", 18

INDEX

Hamburg University, 108
Harley Street, London, 43
Harry Edwards and his Healing, 50
healing gift, the, 22
Healing Intelligence, The, 34, 67
healing service, Haarlem, Holland, 51
Healing Spirit, The, 82
heartburn, 107

incurable diseases, 48, 57, 75, 76, 77, 80, 90, 102, 104, 130, 132, 136, 137, 143–4, 147, 155
infantile paralysis, 57
infertility, 54
Inglefield, Mrs. Freda, 133
Institute for Experimental Medicine, 107

Kermanshah, 21
Kingston Hospital, 111
King's Hall, Manchester, 118

leukaemia, 98, 130
Limacher, Rudi, 114–17
Lister, 69, 76, 77

manipulation, 72, 74, 92
Marley Nursing Home, 48
medical prejudice, 33–34, 59–60, 87, 101, 102, 138, 148,
mediumship, 23, 26, 156–7
mental disease, 111–3, 81
Mesopotamian Expeditionary Force, 15
migraine, 41
morphia, 29
Moorfields, Eye Hospital, 149

Mulfic, Dr. Mahmoud B.Sc., M.D., 107

National Federation of Spiritual Healers, 150, 152
Nelson's Column, Trafalgar Square, 1964, 82
nephritis, 131
Newland, Mrs., 24

Olsen, Mr., 99
Over, Dr. W. P., 45

Paddington Hospital, 108
pancreatitis, 108
paralysis, 45, 81, 82, 89, 93, 94–95, 99, 120, 142
Park Royal Hospital, 137
Pasteur, 69, 76, 77
personal experiences, 98
Peterborough Citizen and Advertiser, 58
pneumonia, 38
poliomeningitis, 82
Poulton, Stanley, 156
Press, 94, 122, 150
Princesses of Greece, 41
Princess Marie Louise, 36–39
Psychic News, 59

radiotherapy, 104, 121
religious prejudice, 19, 148
Royal Albert Hall, 118–22, 137, 155
Royal Engineers, 16
Royal Festival Hall, 93–94, 121
Royal Masonic Hospital, Brighton, 100–1

INDEX

Royal South Hampshire Hospital, 102

Sanctuary, Burrows Lea, Shere, Surrey, 36, 39, 45, 50, 68, 77, 79, 115, 134, 138, 143, 140, 150, 151, 152
Schumann, Robert, 155–6
scorpion sting, 23
Searle, Mr., 121–2
Sellars, John, 96
sinus, 74
skin eruption, 140
slipped disc, 45, 90, 138
spinal collapse, 99
spinal curvature, 32–35, 58, 79, 100, 127
spine, poker-back, 43, 44, 93
spirit communication, 156
Spiritual Healer, The, 62, 66
spirit travelling, 76
St. Bartholomew's Hospital, 98
St. George's Chapel, Windsor, 39
St. John's Ambulance Brigade, 119

St. John's Hospital, Chelmsford, 104
streptococci mastitis, 63
St. Thomas's Hospital, 25
Sycosis Barbae, 48
surgery, 58, 61, 119

thrombosis, 69
tracheotomy, 94
True Magazine, 123
tuberculosis, 24, 85

Unden, Mrs., 115

valvular disease, 133
varicose ulcer, 49
varicose veins, 50
venereal disease, 53
V1 bomb, 88–89
Victoria Halls, Bloomsbury, 82
Vivian, Dr. M., 48–50

war service, 15